A HISTORY OF EARLIEST ITALY

A HISTORY OF EARLIEST ITALY

MASSIMO PALLOTTINO

Translated by Martin Ryle
and Kate Soper

London

First published in English in the UK by
Routledge 1991
11 New Fetter Lane
London EC4P 4EE

Originally published in Italian as *Storia della Prima Italia*

Typeset by Speedset, Ellesmere Port
Printed and bound in Great Britain
by Biddles Ltd, Guildford

British Library Cataloguing in Publication Data
Pallottino, Massimo
  The history of earliest Italy.
  1. Italian civilisation to A.D. 500
  I. Title   II. Storia della prima italia. *English*
  937'.01

ISBN 0 415 05469 9

Contents

5. **Roman Unification and Italic Continuity**

Plates 1–36 between pages 94 and 95

Biographical Note

Massimo Pallottino was born in Rome in 1909. He received his degree from the University of Rome and began his scientific career as an archaeological officer attached to the Department of Antiquities and Fine Arts. In 1940 he was appointed Professor of archaeology and history of Greek and Roman art at Cagliari University, and in 1945 became Professor of Etruscology and Italian antiquities at Rome University.

Though his interests span the entire field of classical archaeology, and even include some aspects of oriental antiquity, Pallottino's speciality has always been the study of the Etruscan world and more generally the history of Italy prior to its romanisation. He has developed Etruscology into a modern integrated discipline including within its compass such diverse aspects as archaeology, art, history and linguistics. He has directed numerous excavations, in particular at Veio and in the Etruscan sanctuary at Pyrgi (Santa Severa), where he discovered the famous gold plaques with bilingual Etruscan and Phoenician inscriptions.

He has established an international reputation as a scholar and is the author of upwards of a hundred publications, of which the following in particular deserve mention: *Elementi di lingua etrusca* 1936; *Tarquinia*, 1937; *Etruscologia*, which appeared in a lengthy series of editions and translations 1942–1984; *L'Arco degli Argentari*, 1946; *Etruscan Painting*, 1952; *Testimonia linguae Etruscae*, 1954 and 1968; *Che cos'è l'archeologia?*, in three editions from 1964 to 1980; *La civiltà artistica etrusco-italica*, 1970; *La langue étrusque*, 1978; *Saggi di antichità*, 1979; *Genti e culture dell'Italia preromana*, 1981.

Massimo Pallottino continues to dedicate a considerable part of his activities to the promotion and organisation of studies, to international scientific cooperation, and to the care and preservation of the Italian and European archaeological heritage. A Fellow of the Accademia dei Lincei of the German Archaeological Institute, the Archaeological Institute of America and a member of the Institut de France, he has been asked to participate in the work of numerous other Italian and foreign scientific institutes. He has received honorary degrees from the universities of Montpellier, Louvain and Strasbourg. In 1982 he was awarded the Balzan Prize, and in 1984 the Erasmus Prize.

Preface

The present work had its origins in the Thomas Spencer Jerome lectures given at Rome and Ann Arbor (Michigan) in 1968. Their publication was delayed, in part through personal circumstances but above all because the years that immediately followed saw a sudden upsurge in archaeological discoveries and critical discussion bearing more or less directly on their subject matter. A considerable updating of the text thus became indispensable. However, this new material did not alter the basic argument, whose outline and development remain faithful to the original plan. The intervening years have, of course, afforded numerous occasions for the author to rehearse the argument and its perspectives: these have included the eighth *Convegno di studi sulla Magna Grecia* at Taranto (a paper on 'La Magna Grecia e l'Etruria', and subsequent contributions to discussion: see the *Atti* of the conference, Naples 1969, pp. 33–48, 250–255); an essay, 'Sul concetto di storia italica', published in *Mélanges offerts à Jacques Heurgon. L'Italie préromaine et la Rome républicaine*, Rome 1976, pp. 771–789; and more recently the article 'L'Italia prima della romanizzazione: proposta di una sintesi storica', which concludes the volume *Popoli e civiltà dell'Italia antica*, VII, Rome 1978, pp. 371–390. The text here placed before the scholarly world, and if possible before a wider audience too, is thus the fruit of a long-considered project, enriched by subsequent labour and reflection, and now ready for the press.

My aim here is to give substance to a new conception of Italy's significance in the Mediterranean world during the first millennium BC. I have tried to consider, or reconsider, the varied phenomena and events of the period within a unified framework, whereas hitherto they have generally been treated in a piecemeal manner, in archaeological, linguistic and ethnographic monographs, concerning particular peoples and cultures, considered in relative isolation and relegated to the margins of Greek and Roman history. Emphasising the inter-relation of these phenomena and events and their connection with major external factors, and identifying their common development, acknowledges the existence, within certain limits, of a historical cycle specific to the Italian area before its unification under Roman rule, and independent of Greek and Roman history. This in turn fills a void in the history of antiquity and outlines the first chapter of the history of Italy. We would argue that such an approach to the past is all the more interesting and all the more relevant to the present in that pre-Roman Italy constitutes the soil in which the country's regional identities took firm root. Over the centuries, these regional identities have repeatedly shown themelves in dialectical opposition to Italy's national vocation.

The intention has been not just to open up a fresh critical perspective, nor simply to 'describe' facts already familiar from other viewpoints, but above all to 'relate' these facts, in their own order and sequence, as a proper historical narrative. Indeed, the very novelty of my critical perspective suggested that the development of the material would be more clearly understood if a fairly comprehensive framework was adopted. Our exposition is intended as far as possible to be plain, clear, and within the grasp of any educated reader. We have avoided superfluous technical detail, and, particularly, technical terminology. The bibliography gives all the references needed by a reader wishing to assess the argument or to explore the subject in greater depth.

The illustrations have been chosen strictly for their usefulness and their relevance to the historical intention of the text – not to provide pretentious and unnecessary 'decoration'. The historical maps have been prepared with particular care, and have been redrawn especially for the present work in the light of our most recent knowledge. The author wishes to express his sincere thanks, for help received in locating the illustrative material, to Dr Maria Paola Baglione, to Professor Franco Panvini Rosati, and, of course, to his publishers.

Warm thanks are owed also to Mrs Sybille Haynes in Oxford, for her invaluable help in revising the English text.

1
Defining 'Italic History'

1

Defining 'Italic History'

Defining 'Italy'

The expression 'pre-Roman Italy' is generally understood to refer to the Italy of antiquity before its political, juridical, linguistic and cultural unification by the Romans (and Rome itself, in the early phases of its own history, was a part of this entity). This is the subject of the present study, and it will be useful to proceed at once to clarify its essential characteristics.

Let us start by outlining the geographical and chronological boundaries of our theme. The term 'Italy' refers to a concept quite familiar to us today, but which nonetheless only acquired its historical meaning with the Roman conquest, or in other words with the formal extension as far as the Alps of the unified Romano-Italic political realm, a project planned by Caesar and completed in 42 BC. Only during the late Imperial period were the three large Mediterranean islands, Sicily, Sardinia and Corsica, included in this realm. We know that in the period before Romanisation there did exist a vague geographical notion of 'Italy', and this became gradually more definite (between the fifth and the third centuries BC) as the name 'Italy' came to be used of the entire peninsula rather than just of the *Mezzogiorno*. Until the annexation of Cisalpine Gaul, or in other words northern Italy, the term continued to refer only to the peninsula, although writers of the Hellenistic period had already begun to regard the Alpine crescent as the true natural outer limit of the *terra Italiae*. We shall apply it to the whole of mainland Italy, and consider also the islands – especially Sicily, which from prehistoric times has had the closest geographical and cultural affinities with the peninsula.

The starting-point for a 'history' of ancient Italy must obviously be the moment at which we can see some traces of historical events in the echoes of tradition and in the earliest surviving written documents. Such evidence, unavailable for the more distant prehistoric ages whose only memorials are material artefacts, exists and can be studied from the late Bronze Age onwards. It becomes more abundant from the early Iron Age, or in other words during the last centuries of the second and the first centuries of the first millennia BC. At this time, the first influences of more highly developed eastern Mediterranean civilisations were beginning to penetrate the territory of Italy, and the ethnic and cultural structures familiar from historical sources were gradually taking shape. These structures endured until the Romanisation of Italy, and here our story ends. But this ending can be given no precise chronological term, since only by a gradual process did Rome impose its hegemony on the entire peninsula during the third century and accomplish complete unity during the first century BC.

Having established the geographical and chronological boundaries of pre-Roman Italy, we must acknowledge that we cannot fully understand what happened there in terms of an integrated, well-defined image. We can form such a picture of the contemporaneous world of the Greeks, which was the expression of a single racial stock with its own character, coherent pattern of development, and unified tradition. Pre-Roman Italy, by contrast, was an admixture of peoples without any common origin, language or culture, whose levels of development differed widely. Moreover, it gives a general impression of receptivity rather than of creativity. It was in many respects linked and indeed subordinate to the civilisations of other areas, influenced and settled by peoples from elsewhere, both from the Mediterranean (where Greek colonisation was of the first importance) and from continental Europe. This is why it has always been so difficult to understand, and why its nature seems so elusive; and this is why the study of pre-Roman Italy is split among so many separate disciplines – the province of prehistorians, classical archaeologists, linguists and historians of religion or art, as well, of course, as of the Greek and Roman historian.

The writers of antiquity clearly realised that beneath the unity of Roman Italy there lay an extremely complex ethnic and historical reality. We find in their works a record of the various Italian peoples, with their names, their territories, and their characteristics. We also find a clear reflection of this reality, or at any rate of how it appeared during its final phase around the time of the completion of the Roman conquest, in the administrative sub-divisions effected by Augustus immediately after Roman unification. These eleven subdivisions bore the traditional geographical and ethnic names: I, Latium et Campania; II, Apulia, Calabria, Salentini et Hirpini; III, Lucania et Bruttii; IV, Sabini et Samnium; V, Picenum; VI, Umbria; VII, Etruria; VIII, Aemilia (= Gallia Cispadana); IX, Liguria; X, Venetia et Histria; XI, (Gallia) Transpadana. Moreover, there was an awareness of the country's links, along its margins, with areas overseas – a further instance of how the geographical terrain of Italy lacked unity and autonomy: for the area of the Mezzogiorno colonised by the Greeks, being known as *Magna Graecia*, was felt to belong to the Greek world also, while the northernmost region, with its Celtic population, was regarded as a part of the Gallic world and called *Gallia Cisalpina*.

If we turn to historical sources to illuminate this complex landscape, we have at our disposal only the literature, Greek and Latin, of classical antiquity, which is no more than a partial and imperfect aid. This is of direct relevance (despite the limitations resulting from the loss of some especially pertinent works) to our knowledge of two areas or aspects of the subject – first, the sphere of Greek colonisation (along the peninsular littoral and also, inseparably, in Sicily), both in its internal development and in its external relationship with the rest of the Hellenic world; and secondly, the history of Rome, which progressively expands from its origins in the heart of Italy until it embraces the entire country. Outside these two zones of light, all our evidence is shadowy, indirect, fragmentary: we owe it to the geographical and ethnographic curiosity of Greek writers, and to the interest of Roman historiographers in the peoples and cultures with which Rome increasingly came into contact. On the other hand, the Roman conquest and the imposition of Latin civilisation and the Latin language led to the complete disappearance of indigenous records (we have in mind especially the literature of the Etruscans), and as a result we have no unbroken link with the historical tradition of a large part of pre-Roman Italy. If we wish to make good this deficiency, at least to some limited extent, we must bring together the various traces found in archaeological remains, in inscriptions and epigraphic documents generally, and in the rather sparse references in the classical sources we have just referred to.

These circumstances explain why the study of the territory of Italy in pre-Roman times, its cultures and their development, has rarely been a central feature of histories of antiquity. Only certain aspects have attracted attention, and then only from certain points of view. The stories of Magna Graecia and of Sicily (in the context of Greek history), of Rome (as the first chapter of Roman history), of the Etruscans and, when they are considered at all, of the other indigenous races and communities have, in other words, been approached as isolated historical themes and problems. Otherwise this world, in all its variety, has almost always been considered in its relation to Rome, as a kind of preparation for Roman culture. The result is that every study of Roman history tends to discuss pre-Roman Italy in its introductory pages, this preliminary discussion being all too often the last we hear of the matter.

There have, however, been advocates of a different approach. They have pointed out that behind the actual multiplicity and diversity of the facts, and despite the uneven quality and availability of the evidence, we can discern common traditions and preoccupations, mutual influences, links across time and space between the different peoples and centres of civilisation, general trends of development and similar cultural forms. Historians would therefore be justified in attempting to establish that these 'first Italians' constituted a culture that was, within certain limits, unified and autonomous. This idea took shape at the beginning of the modern era, and has reappeared with increasing insistence in twentieth-century scholarship. The present volume, proceeding with all critical caution and taking account of the most recent studies, attempts to assess its validity by adopting it, for the first time in contemporary historiography, as the basis for its exposition and narrative.

Giuseppe Micali and nineteenth-century historical thought

It was at the end of the eighteenth and the beginning of the nineteenth centuries that modern scientific historical scholarship began to define its basic approach to the world of classical antiquity. This period saw the publication of the two works generally held to mark the real beginnings of the subjects of 'Greek history' and 'Roman history', namely, W. Mitford's *History of*

Greece (1784–1810) and G. B. Niebuhr's *Römische Geschichte* ('Roman History') (1811–1832). During these same years, however – and scholars seem to have missed the significance of this – Giuseppe Micali published his works, *L'Italia avanti il dominio di Roma* ('Italy before Roman Domination', 1810, but Micali was at work on this text from as early as 1790) and the still more significantly entitled *Storia degli antichi popoli italiani* ('History of the Ancient Italian Peoples', 1832).

Micali's works have been regarded as mere monuments of eighteenth-century antiquarianism, with its exaltation of things Etruscan and Italic in general. They are seen as the final flowering of a tradition unacquainted with the newly established methods of scientific history. This judgement is simply an echo of the negative criticisms made during the nineteenth century, from Niebuhr onwards. It is time to return to Micali's work and to read it more carefully and sympathetically, acknowledging its substantial merits – the breadth of the design, the systematic treatment of the material, the care with which the data are established, the sophistication of the argument. Indeed, the earlier book, which is the more original, already provides a description of the different ethnic groups, including the world of the Greek colonies; a general examination of institutions, economics, culture and language; and a sketch of the sequence of events from the beginnings up to the Roman conquest. The author openly acknowledges the need for critical judgement in sifting through the traditions of antiquity, and he uses as historical sources data drawn from archaeology and from inscriptions: the 'evidence of monuments' and the 'authority of writers' are given equal weight. Moreover, Micali shows a marked inclination, in which he is ahead of his time, to understand history as the outcome of environmental, economic and social conditions. Even the underlying anti-Roman sentiment, already perceptible in eighteenth-century writings, takes on some historio-graphical value insofar as it expresses, if only in emotional terms, the need to claim an autonomous chronological, cultural and political space for the experience of those who lived in Italy before its subjection to Rome.

Micali's work differed from the mass of previous and indeed contemporary historical scholarship, even if it shared and repeated the same ideological bias in favour of Italic values, a bias which in any case flourished in the romantic and nationalistic climate of the

Italian *Risorgimento*. It deserves to take its place in any survey of its period, alongside the great historiographical treatises of the day, such as those by Mitford and Niebuhr. Micali, like these other scholars, sought to explore one of the great sectors of the 'reality' of classical antiquity. Thus, the themes of Greece, Italy and Rome all emerged at the same moment, and as part of the same advance in historical scholarship.

How, though, were they to fare in later years? During the nineteenth century, the great streams of Greek history and Roman history flowed continuously, swelling to the point where they covered the whole field of *Altertumswissenschaft*, the classical scholarship of the positivist and post-positivist period. 'Italic history', by contrast, dwindled and dried up. This is why the works of Mitford and Niebuhr are still regarded as the foundation of a living historiographical tradition, while those of Micali have been forgotten. They are filed with the dead letters of a literature now regarded as pre-scientific, beyond the furthest range of critical or bibliographical curiosity.

The primary reason for the success of Greek and Roman history, as notions and as academic disciplines, has of course been the fact that there exist literary sources from Greek and Latin classical antiquity. Nineteenth-century historical method, with its strong philological bias, saw history as essentially and even exclusively bound up with the use and interpretation of these sources. Other considerations, also linked to the temper of the period, played their part. The prevailing conception of classical historiography saw the historian's essential task as the chronicling of political, military, and biographical facts and events, which reflected the deeds of the dominant classes and important people seen as particularly worthy of record. Nationalist ideology favoured classification in terms of the development of particular ethnic groups: a 'history of peoples'. Analogies with the natural sciences, finally, led to the adoption of biologistic and evolutionary models. All these factors combined to form the character of the two great historiographical 'blocs', Greek history and Roman history. The idea of a history of pre-Roman Italy, by contrast, ran counter to such principles: there was no original, unified historiographical tradition, the existing evidence was for the most part archaeological and bore witness to living conditions and cultural mores rather than to outstanding events, there was an absence of both national unity and evolutionary continuity. The fact that the themes set forth by Micali at the beginning of the nineteenth century were not subsequently developed was not a matter of chance, then, but the logical consequence of a scholarly approach which tended implicitly to reject their conceptual validity.

The history of the Italic world, insofar as it became the object of studies based on the evidence of classical literature, was split between Greek and Roman history. In practice, this meant the history of the Greek littoral of southern Italy and Sicily, and of the Roman monarchy and republic. Whatever lay outside this geographical and chronological area – in other words, everything else relevant to the experience of Italy's indigenous inhabitants – was left almost entirely to the descriptive and reconstructive labours of archaeologists and linguists, who remained within the boundaries of their specialist disciplines (even if the scope of these grew greatly as new discoveries were made and a more sophisticated critical method was developed). Their studies were protohistorical ethnography or anthropology, rather than history as such. Admittedly, within this overall framework a special prominence was of course accorded to the Etruscans, as being by far the most important of all the non-Hellenic peoples of Italy. Nonetheless, Etruscan studies, despite the relatively abundant data available from tradition and from inscriptions, never developed into a truly historical discipline. It was seen essentially as research into Etruscan civilisation in terms of its monuments, art, religion, customs, language and so forth.

For almost a hundred years, then – and these years saw great and unprecedented progress in the rediscovery of classical antiquity – the problems of pre-Roman Italy were more or less denied any intrinsic 'historicity'. Their study remained 'underdeveloped' by comparison with what was achieved during the same period in studies of the Greek and Roman world. The collection, analysis, interpretation and antiquarian understanding of the data recalls the piecemeal erudition of the eighteenth century. That such a state of affairs continued for so long, despite the advances of modern criticism, is explained above all by the prestige of establishment scholarship, especially German and German-language scholarship. Its dogmatic assumptions were often intolerantly imposed even in questions of methodology. Everything was judged by the touchstone of Greek civilisation (a tendency which found its culmination and epitome in the neo-humanism of Helmut Berve), and the result was a lack of interest in, not to say contempt for, whatever was 'not Greek' and 'not classical'.

New directions: the Rome-Italy dialectic

At the beginning of the present century, the historical conception of pre-Roman Italy still reflected the attitudes we have described; indeed, it has continued to do so in many respects right up to the present. But reasons for dissent and signs of reaction have inevitably become apparent, especially in recent decades. There has been a continuous and swelling stream of archaeological and epigraphic discovery bearing on the civilisation of the Etruscans and of the other peoples and communities who lived in the Italian area, including the Greek colonies. As a result, it has become gradually but incontrovertibly clear that the experience of these people has great significance, qualitatively and quantitatively, in any overall assessment of the historical and cultural development of antiquity. It is less and less acceptable to relegate it to the margins and consider it piecemeal.

Moreover, classical studies themselves have significantly changed and developed, and now differ very considerably from the original nineteenth-century model. Historians of antiquity are increasingly inclined to go beyond reinterpreting the information and narratives found in classical literature, and have made more and more use of all the various possible sources of knowledge: inscriptions, coins, monuments, drawings and figurative art. The range of their interests has broadened to include the reconstruction of social and economic conditions, modes of life, technical developments, customs. Above all, the concept of the history of nations has given way to new and different perspectives – universal history; histories of particular periods and environments, social groups, or cultural phenomena; and so forth. In every sphere of historical and social anthropological research, there has been a marked reaction against evolutionary and deterministic models. And so, one by one, the main conceptual barriers have been coming down, until the way lies open to what was unattainable in the nineteenth century: a unified and distinct history of pre-Roman Italy.

Given all this, it is not surprising that Micali's project has found a newly receptive audience, even if only in the sense that the development of modern historical scholarship has necessarily implied a more mature and subtle critical and self-critical scrutiny.

The question of relations between Italy and Rome has been especially important here. Traditionally, Roman history was treated diachronically, as the history of the continuous development of Rome, from its beginnings until it achieved universal dominion. The rest of the Italian world appeared 'foreign' – subsidiary to the sole focus of interest, Rome. It was seen from the exclusively Roman perspective of the Latin annalists and historians themselves. But Rome was a part of the Italic world, a simple truth of which the ancients themselves were quite aware, and which modern critical thought has grasped. We have already noted that although the historians of antiquity had an idea of Italy as distinct from Rome, their notion of Italy was also in fact identified with the extension of Rome's dominion. In the special circumstances of the 'Social Wars' of the early first century BC, the difference of emphasis amounted to an outright contradiction. Later, above all in the political and ideological climate of the Augustan period, the contradiction was softened. As we know from Virgil's epic, a benign destiny was thought to smile upon relations between Rome and Italy, guaranteeing continuity and fulfilment on both sides. Italy became an 'internal' and essential factor in the history of Rome, as did Rome in Italy's history. The pattern of classical thinking may illuminate modern attitudes to the same problem. We are now more willing to take account of the values of the Italic world as formative historical factors. 'Italy' is no longer simply the source of useful data: we strive to avoid the rigidly Roman-centred perspectives of nineteenth-century historical method.

It is worth noting that as early as the mid-nineteenth century Theodor Mommsen declared, in his famous *Römische Geschichte* ('Roman History') that he wanted to recount not so much the history of Rome as the history of Italy, in that Rome had given form to the Italic 'material'. Mommsen definitely understood the Rome-Italy dialectic as a relation of complementarity – a point of view not very different from that of the Romans of the Augustan period, and in direct contrast to the perspective of Micali, who saw the relation as one of fracture and antithesis. But this was an isolated, and purely theoretical, moment in the context of the methodology and narrative procedure typical of a 'history of Rome' written altogether in the spirit of its time.

It was at the beginning of the present century that it first became possible, and thinkable, to reconsider Roman history, above all in its earliest phases, in the light thrown by linguistic and archaeological evidence about other Italian peoples, and to reconstruct a network of common conditions and processes and mutual influences. This type of evidence has certainly not been comparable in scope or extent to the great wealth of material directly embodied in Roman historiographical tradition. Nonetheless, it has proved invaluable, and sometimes indeed of decisive importance, in confirming, modifying, refining and enlarging the knowledge derived from critical study of the literary sources.

One early example of the systematic use of non-Latin (and especially Etruscan) inscriptions, in connection with an issue – namely, the origins of Latin personal names – involving Roman-Italic 'exchange', is W. Schulze's work *Zur Geschichte lateinischer Eigennamen* ('On the History of Latin Names': 1904). It was in research into the history of the laws and institutions of Rome during the regal and republican eras, however, that the ever-growing volume of inscriptions, Etruscan, Umbrian and Oscan, at once newly discovered, authentic and chronologically contemporary (even if often difficult to interpret), helped to revitalise, if not indeed to revolutionise, existing scholarship. The first example was A. Rosenberg's *Der Staat der alten Italiker* ('The State in Ancient Italic Societies': 1913), which subordinated the narrowly Rome-centred problematic to a common Italic perspective. This marked the opening of a long scholarly debate that has drawn contributions from a range of disciplines (studies of inscriptions, of language and philology; historico-cultural research; juridical and sociological enquiry, and so on), seen the polemical pendulum swing to the side now of Rome and now of Italy, led through a maze of subtle and complex discussions and hypotheses (above all, of late, concerning the passage from monarchy to republic), and involved an illustrious company of historians and jurists from many nations, who include E. Kornemann, F. Leifer, H. Rudolf, E. Meyer, L. Pareti, P. Fraccaro. S. Mazzarino, A. Alföldi, A. Momigliano, P. De Francisci, F. De Martino, J. Heurgon, R. E. A. Palmer and J.-C. Richard. Similar perspectives have been developed in the study of links between the earliest Roman religions and Italic cults, and of other problems, such as the recent theme of the emergence of the city.

The 1920s saw a sudden and general quickening of interest in the civilisations of pre-Roman Italy. On one hand, Etruscan studies, stimulated by new archaeological investigations and discoveries such as those at Veii and Caere (Cervèteri), advanced decisively in every field: consideration of the Etruscans' origins, investigation of their language, attempts to distinguish what made Etruscan figurative art original and distinct from the art of the Greeks. Work on the Etruscans was the focus of international scholarly conferences and established itself in permanent research institutes, becoming part of European culture. On the other hand, aspects of the culture of the various Italic peoples, apart from the Etruscans, also began to be considered, in such massive and systematic works as F. von Duhn's *Italische Gräberkunde* (1923). A new understanding of the Greeks in Italy was developing during this same period, as a result of Paolo Orsi's impressive findings at sites in Magna Graecia and Sicily and of the contributions made by such historians as G. Giannelli and E. Ciaceri. This was a prelude to the great flourishing of projects, excavation and scholarly debate in this field since the Second World War.

All this led to a further decisive growth in awareness of the importance of the whole Italic world, in which traditional historiography had shown so little interest. Thus, the single year of 1925 saw three events of crucial importance, namely the publication of E. Pais' *Storia dell'Italia antica* ('History of Ancient Italy') and L. Homo's *L'Italie primitive et les débuts de l'impérialisme romain* ('Primitive Italy and Early Roman Imperialism'), and, above all, the lecture given at Florence, under the title of 'Storia Italica' ('Italic History'), by Ulrich von Wilamowitz-Moellendorf.

We shall shortly see that the position taken by Wilamowitz was particularly significant for the history of the problem we are discussing. Scholars were by now clearly inclined to treat the whole of the earlier phase of Roman history, up to the unification of the peninsula, as an Italic-Roman history – a territory shared between the two historical perspectives of Italy and Rome. As in Mommsen, Italy is seen as a rather static, conditioning medium for the innovatory dynamism of Rome. This applies, not only to the works of Pais and Homo, but also to many valuable later studies, such as those by K. J. Beloch, F. Altheim (explicitly entitled, in the original 1941 edition, *Italien und Rom*: 'Italy and Rome') and L. Pareti. These works show a fully developed sense both of the indissoluble links between Rome and the communities which surrounded it, and of those between non-Hellenic and Greek Italy – a sense succinctly expressed in S. Mazzarino's suggestion that we should think in terms of a Greco-Italic-Roman *koiné*.

However, even these scholars see the Rome-Italy dialectic somewhat as it was seen in classical Augustan ideology: the fate of Italy is sealed in the last analysis by the 'miracle' of Rome, which brings its disparate premises to a single conclusion and is the goal of its common striving. Mazzarino, for example, writes that the experience of the Italic peoples 'reaches out towards the future' and 'takes on meaning only in terms of Rome'. This amounts to declaring that their doings, unless passed through the Roman filter, are of purely academic interest and have no historical status. These themes and beliefs, this notion of Italy as the forerunner of Rome, are deep-rooted and persistent. They are reflected, for instance, even in the title of a work expressly devoted to describing the peoples and civilisations of pre-Roman Italy, J. Whatmough's *The Foundations of Roman Italy* (1937), a compendium of the scholarship of the immediately preceding period which has no counterpart up to the present day.

Current approaches

There was a further and radical shift in perspective when it was explicitly suggested that the pluralistic Italic world might be separated from the unity of Rome by a clear line of demarcation, a frontier not just chronological but methodological, which would give legitimacy to the notion of two separate 'histories'. This point of view was first expressed in Wilamowitz's Florence lecture, mentioned above, whose impact was sudden and sensational. The Italic world, declared Wilamowitz, had its own rich and original values of life and civilisation, which were the common heritage of all the various races (the Greeks included) of ancient Italy, and which themselves influenced Rome, before the process of Romanisation led to their extinction. This point of view, explicitly returning to Micali and reaffirming his underlying thesis, broke with and indeed overturned received opinion, for it denied that any evolutionary continuum led from the earliest Italic peoples up to the triumph of Rome. This last was seen as the ending of an earlier historical phase that was complete in itself. Wilamowitz, coining the phrase *storia italica* – 'Italic history' – to express these ideas, issued to the scholarly world an invitation and a challenge: to write a history of the Italic world, based chiefly on the evidence of monumental remains, regarded no longer as of merely analytic and descriptive archaeological interest but as authentic historical sources which were to take the place, in this particular cultural and chronological field, of literary sources. This was to proclaim – or to reclaim, on a more secure critical basis – the validity and autonomy of the data about the pre-Roman Italian world, and to ward off the bias of Roman historiography with its *a posteriori* vision.

Wilamowitz's suggestion, bold and in a sense provocative as it was, had no immediate effect. His invitation met with no swift response. Indeed, the present book may claim to be the first direct answer to his challenge. Then and afterwards, historical criticism continued to interest itself chiefly in the history of Rome, or in Italic-Roman history seen (along the lines we have noted) as an indissoluble whole. The fact that Wilamowitz was not a historian but a philologist may partly explain this muted response. In fact, his new approach first had an (admittedly uneven) influence among archaeologists and linguists. Amedeo Maiuri, in his essay 'Problemi di archeologia italica' ('Problems of Italic Archaeology': 1946), invoked Micali and Wilamowitz in support of his argument for using the rich harvest gleaned from uncovering the civilisations of ancient Italy. Giacomo Devoto (among others) made similar points, writing in the Preface to the second edition of his *Gli antichi Italici* ('The Ancient Italic Peoples': 1951) of the need to 'draw a modern picture of ancient Italy seen through non-Roman eyes'. Eventually, even the historian Giulio Giannelli – if only in the retrospective review of studies in Roman history which forms the Introduction to his *Trattato di storia romana* ('Roman History') (volume I, 1953) – announced that he thought it right (as Micali and Wilamowitz had done) to regard Italic history as autonomous, and deplored the 'erroneous framework' imposed by traditional historiography.

This substantially revised point of view has been the basis for much recent and contemporary concrete work – new lines of research and publication dealing with particular historical, institutional and cultural themes and problems of pre-Roman Italy. This work shows a growing tendency to juxtapose, compare, interpret within a single framework, and even at times assimilate data on more or less contemporaneous events and phenomena in what had hitherto been regarded as the separate milieux of Magna Graecia, Rome, Etruria and so forth. These discussions have dealt with issues that have lately aroused keen interest, in the wake of several remarkable archaeological discoveries, especially those of inscriptions.

For example, there has been an ever-increasing volume of finds dating from the late Bronze Age, including examples of Mycenaean pottery scattered throughout Italy. Above all, much material has been recovered relating to the so-called 'proto-Villanovan' cultures of the late Bronze Age. From these discoveries, from Iron Age finds (especially those excavated in the necropolises of Latium), and also from examination of the sites of the earliest Greek colonies such as Pithecusae on Ischia and Megara Hyblaea in Sicily, it is becoming ever clearer that there are extremely close connections between what we can observe of the earliest periods of civilisation in the various territorial and cultural areas of proto-historical Italy. This led the present author to survey the field, as further illuminated by data obtained from classical tradition, in a unified interpretative framework in an essay on 'Le origine storiche dei popoli italici' ('Historical Origins of the Italic Peoples': 1955).

A new enthusiasm has enlivened discussion of the relations between Rome, Magna Graecia and and Etruria — for instance, in the work of F. Sartori and D. van Berchem, in the contributions to the 1968 Taranto Conference on 'Magna Graecia and Rome in Archaic Times', and in the scholarly meeting held in 1977 in the Campidoglio at Rome, whose theme was 'Latium in Archaic Times and the Greek World'. More generally, it has been emphasised that we need a unified understanding of the archaic civilisation of the Greco-Tyrrhenian area (where the term 'Tyrrhenian' is taken to cover the coastal strip from Campania up through Latium to Etruria), as implied in Mazzarino's *koiné*, when we approach such questions as the development and governance of the city-states modelled on the Greek *polis*, religion, intellectual and material life, customs, artistic trends, and so on. The discovery of the Pyrgi gold plaque inscriptions has been crucial. They have given rise to extensive commentaries, not only among students of inscriptions and of the Etruscan and Semitic languages, but in the entire field of the history of antiquity. They have shed new and unexpected light on the relations of the Etruscans with the outside world at the close of the archaic period, and on institutional forms and processes in Etruria as these may relate to Rome and the Greek colonies. Comparative historico-religious research into the cults of Magna Graecia, Rome and Etruria has made great progress lately. G. Pugliese Carratelli has been among the pioneers, and here too archaeological discoveries, especially those made in excavations at Rome (in particular in the ancient temple of S. Omobono) and at Lavinium, have provoked lively discussion. Paintings in the tomb known as the tomb of the Tuffatore, which dates from the early decades of the fifth century BC and which was discovered in the necropolis at Paestum, have provided particularly significant evidence that the funeral customs of the Greeks of Posidonia had much in common, ideologically and iconographically, with those of the Etruscans of Tarquinii. In fashion and costume, at more or less the same time, we might note the correspondence (which I commented on at the time of the discovery) between an item in the 'chronicles of Cumae' cited by Dionysus of Halicarnassus (VII 2ff.) and evidence from the tomb of the Leopardi at Tarquinii concerning the vogue for blonde hair among women, clearly common to Etruria and the Greek colony of Cumae. The detail, of slight importance in itself, is of interest because it was brought to light through the comparison of sources of differing kinds in two different ethnic contexts.

Marta Sordi used similar methods when she brought together data drawn from the Greek, Etruscan and Roman worlds, concerning events of the fifth and fourth centuries BC, in her study of the inter-relationship between the Roman conquest of Veii, the Gallic invasion, and the Italian policy of Dionysius of Syracuse. The same methods were further developed in discussions of the problems posed by another sensational discovery, the finding at Tarquinii of fragmentary Latin inscriptions that included biographical accounts of members of the Etruscan Spurinna family. M. Torelli, in his *Elogia Tarquiniensia* (1975), aimed to place these discoveries in their historical context. He drew on sources in Greek and Roman historiography which dealt with the Athenian expedition against Syracuse at the end of the fifth century BC and with the war between Rome and the Tarquinians in the middle of the fourth century BC; and he further hypothesised that a direct archaeological record of this same Spurinna family was to be found in the Tomb of Orcus I at Tarquinii, with its Etruscan inscriptions and its drawings. Finally, the work of J. Heurgon makes systematic use of Latin literature to portray the deeds, prominent characters and atmosphere of Etruscan life during the Hellenistic and Roman era: see especially the final chapter of his book *La vie quotidienne chez les Etrusques* ('Daily Life among the Etruscans': 1961, but the latest, 1979 edition has an Appendix incorporating subsequent scholarship). Heurgon has stressed the interconnectedness of historical processes amongst the peoples of the land of Italy, as against the old mental habit, derived from the classical annalists, of seeing them as discrete and mutually 'impermeable' (see the 1967 'Entretiens Hardt').

The present revisionist tendency has also affected the study of artistic expression. The traditional rigid division categorised the various series of figurative artefacts in accordance with ethnic preconceptions: there was 'Greek art', 'Etruscan art', 'Roman art', 'Italic art' – and it was not always easy to fit the actual artefacts into this schema. Nowadays, there is a growing preference for more nuanced analytic and interpretative criteria, which, while not neglecting local traditions and customs, take account of the unquestionable fact that mutual influences and common trends linked the non-Hellenic cultures not only with one another but also with the world of the Greek colonies (as had been indicated as early as 1949 by E. Langlotz). The possibility of considering the art of the entire Italic world as constituting, within limits, a coherent whole has recently been demonstrated in surveys by the present author (1971) and by R. Bianchi Bandinelli (1973). The Brussels Europalia exhibition of 1980 adopted this critical perspective explicitly in planning the display entitled 'Prima Italia. Arts italiques du premier millénaire avant J.-C.' ('The First Italians: the Arts of the Italic Peoples during the first millennium BC'), a display subsequently transferred to Rome.

Towards a unified historical image of the Italic world

The time is now ripe for a reinterpretation of the historical material of pre-Roman Italy. The new approach must break with conventional wisdom: not only with the Roman-centred tradition derived from Niebuhr, but also with the current conception of a history oscillating between the two poles of Italy and Rome, which seeks to evoke an Italic world whose destiny lay in its ultimate unification with the Roman world. In other words, we must study the Italic world as such, with its own chronological framework and its own characteristics; and we must acknowledge that it possessed its own overarching identity and course of development, parallel to that of the Greek world during the first millennium BC. It thus represents one 'regional' aspect of the history of antiquity, before that history, in Italy and Greece alike, was absorbed into the universalist self-assertion of Rome. To attempt an organic treatment of this developing theme is to embark after almost two centuries on the project outlined by Micali, and to respond after more than fifty years to Wilamowitz's challenge by relating an authentic Italic history.

It will of course be essential to set out and abide by certain conceptual and methodological criteria. These have already been partly set out in the studies of the last few decades, discussed above, which have followed on the work of Wilamowitz, but it will be helpful to summarise them:

1. *The data and their use*
We shall regard as available for use all sources of information, with associated critical and scholarly commentary, which the traditional disciplines, insofar as they deal with relevant material, make use of. This comprises, on the one hand, the history of Greece in its relations with Italy and of Rome in the age of the kings and the republic, and on the other hand the proto-history of the Italic world: the study of the Etruscans, and archaeological and linguistic research into the other indigenous peoples of the land of Italy. In certain fields, non-Italian studies may also be relevant to Italy. So far as the nature of the evidence is concerned, we shall follow the latest methodological recommendations and practices. Every type of source – not just historiographical, but archaeological and linguistic – must be given equal critical weight, and regarded as equally and (in Devoto's useful phrase) 'impartially' valid when we attempt to establish the historical context.

2. Chronological perspective

It may seem superfluous and even ingenuous to recall that the facts of the past are to be described and understood in the light of what was happening at the time and what had happened earlier, rather than in the light of events yet to take place. Those who follow in the intellectual track of classical writers, seeing the story of pre-Roman Italy as a prologue or even a necessary premise to the grand triumph of Rome, do however run the risk of adopting, instinctively and more or less unconsciously, that kind of *a posteriori* perspective. The truth is that at least until the beginning of the third century BC Rome's eventual role in the Italic world remained an open question: Rome was just one actor, albeit an important one, on a stage where the leading parts were played by the Greeks, the Etruscans, and the Italic peoples who spoke the Osco-Umbrian tongue. And the object of our research is to recapture the texture of this drama, to recall its scope and retrace its plot.

3. Connections between contemporaneous facts

Interconnections of this kind largely escape the attention of those who view history as 'diachronic', as the self-enclosed development over time of particular peoples or states. Nowadays, that kind of approach is in fact being displaced by systematic research into 'epochal' or 'synchronic' links. This has already given valuable results in pioneering work (cited above) by Sordi, Heurgon and others. The links lie in those common conditions, mimetic tendencies, and mutual influences and reactions which must inevitably have existed between neighbours at any given historical moment, and which need rediscovery or highlighting. We have to make some logical and imaginative effort if we are to overcome old mental habits. We easily 'see' some phase of the political, socio-economic or cultural history of Magna Graecia solely in the context of the evolution of the Greek world, discussing and interpreting it in the context of Greek historiographical and archaeological source-materials. We try to resolve some problem of regal or republican Rome in the light of Roman tradition alone, or to assess some aspect of Etruscan civilisation in its purely Etruscan bearings, with no reference to its surroundings in space and time. We interpret the cultural import of this or that necropolis in Latium, Campania, Picenum, the Veneto or elsewhere along lines laid down by archaeological experts in the proto-history of the region in question and in terms of the limited technical, typological and chronological questions arising from their particular interests and from the procedures with which they are most familiar. But we must attempt to break down these conventional barriers between branches of study, or open more fluid communication between them. Only then will we be able to reconstruct a historical reality of whose fundamental interconnections we have so far caught no more than a confused glimpse.

4. Tracing a common process of development
We must adopt a combined, comparative and unitary approach not only to particular phases but to their succession. The sequence of events in pre-Roman Italy, in other words, must be considered in its own appropriate perspective, based on the logic of their spatial and temporal relations and on their particular significance for the development of the world of antiquity. And yet this perspective must differ from those of Greek and Roman history. Here, plainly, is the most delicate conceptual exercise of all: the devising of a real, rather than illusory, framework in which to grasp 'Italic history'. This is the object of the present study, reflected in the identification of a coherent evolutionary process whose essential stages – its origins, its flourishing in the period of antiquity, its crisis, and its persistence into a new order – provide the material for the chapters of historical argument which follow.

2

Origins

2

Origins

The nature of the problem

Ancient and modern thinkers alike have been fascinated by the theme of the origins of the peoples and history of the Italic world. Both ancients and moderns have tried to explain the problem in accordance with what they have known and, above all, with their own habits of mind.

For the ancients, the notion of origins involved precisely known events and identifiable actors. The usual image was of maritime immigration into Italy, to some extent along the lines of the Greek colonisation of historical record, but taking place in an earlier heroic age and carried out by various peoples moving westwards out of the east – Arcadians, Pelasgians, Achaeans, Trojans, Lydians, Cretans, Iapygians – and by heroes who established civilisations and founded cities: Oenotrius, Peucetius, Heracles, Minos, Ulysses, Diomedes, Aeneas, Antenor, Tyrrhenus, and so forth. Though a few episodes, such as the arrival of Oenotrius and the Arcadians, were placed in a more remote past, most of these events were thought to have occurred around the time of the Trojan War. The seizure and occupation of new territories was sometimes symbolically recounted in the tale of the heroic foreigner who first waged war on the indigenous inhabitants and then married the daughter of their king and so inherited his dominions. This fate befell Diomedes in Apulia, where Daunus was king, and Aeneas in Latium, where Latinus reigned. This amounted to acknowledgement that there had been indigenous peoples and new arrivals, and that the historically known races were their joint issue. The origin of cities was thought of as an act of will, a founding moment taking place at a precise time – a concept that parallels the foundation of the actual

Greek colonies. Further internal migration, it was thought, had then engendered new races from the already existing peoples. The Aborigines of central Italy were regarded as the issue of the southern Italian Oenotrians, themselves descended from Oenotrius' Arcadians, while the Aborigines in their turn were believed to have given birth, by way of further fusions, to the Latini.

These various, complicated and sometimes even contradictory narratives are quite clearly derived from 'very old tales' (*palaiotatoi mythoi*). Even the historians of classical times were conscious of their legendary aura, and gave them doubtful credence. The modern critical scholarship of the nineteenth century made short work of them, consigning all but a few exceptions to the realm of myth and fable. Today, however, we are beginning to feel that some of these traditions, corrupt as they may be, hold echoes of a far-off historical reality.

Modern scholarship, even as it rejected the notions of antiquity, remained fixated on the idea that the origins of the Italic peoples were to be found in the effects of immigration from outside, though this was now thought to have followed a different pattern. Comparative linguistics established the original unity of the Indo-European languages, and during the era of positivism this led to the supposition that these languages had been spread by migrant peoples travelling overland from a common territorial starting point. The image was of a great diaspora. The Asiatic Aryans of India and Iran were believed to be related to many of the important European and Mediterranean races – Hittites, Greeks, Italic and Celtic peoples, Germans, Slavs. The starting point of Italic history came to be identified with the moment at which 'the Italic people' crossed over the Alps from continental Europe, entering the plain of the Po valley and moving into the peninsula. We see here, too, the influence of a model derived from later historical events: the expansion of the Celts into pre-Roman Italy, and the barbarian invasions which marked the end of the world of classical antiquity.

Another great enterprise of positivist scholarship, prehistoric archaeology, seemed to confirm and enhance this theory. The arrival of the Italic peoples was discerned in the appearance of Bronze Age civilisation among the northern Italian *terramare* (villages built on piles and protected by dykes and embankments). It was also detected in the spread from north to south of cremation as a funeral rite (this thesis was put forward especially by W. Helbig and L. Pigorini, and is generally associated with the latter). At this time, it was an axiom that aspects of culture revealed by archaeological discovery must have an ethno-linguistic explanation, as summed up in G. Kossinna's 'law' stating that 'each distinct cultural area, however small, must imply a distinct racial stock'. Explanations of this kind encouraged ingenious schemes of historical reconstruction, often simplistic and dogmatically maintained, which ultimately proved inconsistent.

Italy, then, was thought to have been exposed to Indo-European influence in primitive times by way of invasions. Archaeological evidence was thought to prove as much. This was seen as an essential factor in the original historical constitution of the country. The idea has been much developed, clarified and refined, especially in the present century, through the progress of linguistic science and the growing quantity of archaeological finds. It has been realised, for instance, that the various Indo-European languages spoken in Italy in historical times (Latin, Osco-Umbrian, Venetic, Messapian) cannot be regarded as derivatives of a hypothetical 'common Italic tongue', characterised among other features by independent links with other non-Italian Indo-European languages. Archaeologists have held that the cultural changes of the late prehistoric period, from the neolithic to the Bronze and Iron Ages, can be explained in terms of the movement of peoples from territory to territory, and this seems to apply to what we observe in Italy (for instance, in neolithic cultures with their square-mouthed jars or war axes, in pottery with spiral and meander decorations, in the urnfields, and so on). Such movements are thought to have occurred most especially in eastern central Europe where the Indo-Europeans are believed to have principally spread. There have also been attempts to establish a more detailed and exact correspondence between particular cultural innovations and the advent of particular racial groups (the historian L. Pareti, for example, held that the cremating peoples of the late Bronze Age, the so-called 'pre-Villanovan' culture, were the forebears of the eastern Italic people who spoke the Osco-Umbrian language).

The image of a once-and-for-all immigration of 'the Italic people' came to be replaced, then, by a picture of many successive immigratory waves. But the same underlying interpretation was

retained. A new historical cycle was seen as beginning with some
distinct event or events – in the present case, the advent of more or
less ready-constituted ethnic groups from their continental base –
just as the ethnographers of antiquity took as their starting-point
maritime immigrations from the eastern Mediterranean. It is odd
that only in the case of the Etruscans (apart, of course, from the real
historical phenomenon of Greek colonisation) was credence generally given to this classical tradition of an eastern maritime
provenance: the Etruscans were generally identified with the
Lydians led by Tyrrhenus, or else with the Pelasgians. Their
relative linguistic isolation, and other distinctive characteristics,
led rightly or wrongly to the notion that they were separate from
the Indo-European Italic peoples.

This ethno-genetic viewpoint, which informed both the
methods and the results of positivistic scholarship, has been
plunged into crisis as a result of the rapid and extensive growth in
archaeological, linguistic and historical knowledge over the last
few decades. New data have come to light, presenting a more
complex picture often directly at variance with established
theories, giving rise to doubts, and opening up fresh critical
perspectives. The old image of a primitive Italy populated and
civilised by incursions from the north has been turned upside
down by discoveries showing the existence of developed, sophisticated and enduring neolithic cultures in the Italian Mezzogiorno
and the islands; of Bronze Age civilisations of the type dubbed
'Apenninic' spread across the entire peninsula (relegating the
well-known *terramare* to a relatively marginal and chronologically
subordinate position); of marked and repeated influences from the
eastern Mediterranean Orient, which culminated in the presence
of Mycenaean traders, who may even have been in some sense
colonists, in Apulia and the Sicilian region, as well as along the
Tyrrhenian coast and in Sardinia; and of the practice of cremation
in southern Italy at a date no later than it is found in the north. All
this shows the importance, and the early date, of local advances in
the peninsula and the islands, and the significant role played by
contacts and influences from the Mediterranean. Linguistic
research, meanwhile, has come to focus on the substrata – in other
words, on the problems of the tongues spoken by the inhabitants
of Italy in times predating the diffusion of the Indo-European
languages – and has found evidence in the remains surviving in

place-names (whose linguistic conservatism is well known) and above all in the traces left in the vocabulary of the later languages and dialects. These earlier tongues have proved to be many-layered and various, and show links with other, non-Italian areas. Historical study of the Italic Indo-European tongues has moreover gradually revealed that they too show marks of subsequent evolution, the result of a long and complicated gestation combining a range of developments, superimpositions, cross-contaminations (between the various Indo-European branches, and also between the latter and the indigenous substrata) and common innovations: a gestation which took place largely within the territorial confines of Italy before the historical era began.

This changing and widening perspective soon led to a reaction against the old hypotheses in which invasions had played such a central role. Research into the origins of the Italic world attributed less importance to external factors, and more to indigenous ethnic and cultural factors. This approach was especially prevalent between the two World Wars, its principal exponent being G. Patroni. The substitution of Indo-European languages for the earlier substrata, and the adoption of other innovatory trends, were attributed primarily to a gradual and essentially peaceful process of assimilation, in which impulses from outside Italy were absorbed without substantial changes in the original population. A similar thesis held sway at this time in studies of the origins of the Etruscans, with the rejection both of the traditional idea that they had come from the east and of the view that they were of northern provenance (rather as the classical historian Dionysus of Hali-carnassus had thought: cf. I, 30). G. Devoto and others explained the difference between the Etruscan language and the Italic varieties of Indo-European not as resulting from later outside influence, but in terms of the survival, into the historical era, of a relic of the pre-Indo-European substratum.

Leaving aside these more extreme polemical reactions against the 'dogmatism' of those who had given priority to external factors, we can discern, across the wide range of opinions that inform the most recent studies, a considerably more nuanced awareness of the problem of the origins of the Italic world. Various aspects of the question have been studied by, among others, F. Altheim, G. Devoto, A. Furumark, C. F. Hawkes, H. Hencken, G. Kaschnitz-Weinberg, P. Laviosa Zambotti and R. Peroni, while the present author has devoted an essay to the issue as a whole.

The abundance, variety and complexity of the evidence now available incline us today to go beyond the choice, or opposition, between theses of immigration by sea or by land, and between a one-sided emphasis on either invasions or indigenous factors. We can now acknowledge the part that may have been played by maritime 'pre-colonial' settlement, by overland movements of peoples large and small or of isolated groups, by the assimilation of foreign elements, and by commercial and cultural contacts both by the continental land routes of the north and by sea, whether across the Adriatic or by the coastal passages of the Mediterranean used from the dawn of the neolithic age. At the same time, it is recognised that local cultures and populations will have persisted, and developed along lines of their own. The key to a pluralistic understanding of the problem of the formative elements of Italic life lies essentially in the stress that must be placed on the oft-neglected 'time-factor'. We need to see things in their full depth. We must assume a very long and varied succession of events and developments (as we should realise from the analogous example of the thousand-year-long formation of modern Europe), rather than succumbing to our instinctive tendency to produce a simplified and one-dimensional image by picking out and concentrating on a single theme, phenomenon or occurrence. This is the criterion of a fresh approach, more sensitive to historical values, which offers – or should offer – a contrast to the mental habits both of classical antiquity and of previous scholarship in the modern period.

The problem of the origins of the Italic world must, moreover, be posed in a wider context. Hitherto, it has constituted a discrete topic, contained within its own geographical frontiers, studied for the most part only by those concerned with prehistory or linguistics, and regarded almost exclusively from an ethno-genetic standpoint. We must situate it within the historical framework of ancient Mediterranean civilisation. Recent discoveries in the Aegean and the Near East have made this much easier, for they have greatly expanded our knowledge of conditions and events in the eastern Mediterranean during the period of the ripening and development of the societies that gave birth to Italic history. This is not just a question of recognising and interpreting the complex eastern influences felt on Italian soil. We must also accept that the major events of the Oriental world may have played a determining role, either directly or through their repercussions, in forming some of the fundamental structures of Italic history. This may well have been the case, for example, at the time of the great Mycenaean expansion and the period of turbulence and decline that marked the late Bronze Age. It becomes unmistakably evident with the advent of the Greek colonies. We should therefore feel able to make cautious use of historical materials from the Orient (in connection with the possible kinship between the names of the so-called 'peoples of the sea' and the names of peoples inhabiting the land of Italy), and also to reassess the value of the traditional Greek legends about links between the Aegean world and the Italy of primitive times. If not historical sources in the full sense, these are nonetheless clues to be taken into account alongside the archaeo-logical and linguistic data.

Those concerned with the origins of the Italic world increasingly (and in my view rightly) accept that many factors are relevant to the problem, that an in-depth chronological perspective is required, and that an attempt should be made to place things in their broader historical environment. The notion of a 'beginning', a particular moment, is giving way to the notion of 'formation' or 'develop-ment' spread out over time. Scholars no longer pursue the will-o'-the-wisp of a 'point of departure', conceived in deterministic fashion as containing in embryo all future developments, located in the distant past, and identified either with immigrations or with the indigenous cultures. If we use such terms at all, we are more likely to speak of a 'point of arrival' – a moment at which the formative processes of ethnic and cultural life finally coalesce, in the sense intended by U. Rellini when he said (speaking, precisely, of the birth of the Italic peoples) that 'the *ethnos* comes into being gradually, over a long period'. Nor is it now thought reasonable to trace the existence, for example, of a Latin or Etruscan nation or civilisation back beyond this 'point of arrival', seeking them (as they were once sought) in far-off times and places – any more than it would be thought reasonable for a historian of the modern period to ingenuously posit a French nation or civilisation *avant la lettre* and to identify it with the Celts, the peoples of Roman Gaul, the Franks, the Visigoths, the Burgundians or the Normans.

The study of the origins of Italy as it appeared on the threshold of the historical period thus presents contemporary scholarship with two distinct if intimately related tasks. On the one hand, it involves research into and analysis of the formative elements – ethnic, linguistic and cultural, indigenous or exotic, disparate or cognate – which came together in the prehistoric formative period. On the other, it requires us to identify and interpret the processes which shaped that period's historical conclusion.

It is of course important to bear in mind the fundamental difference between Italy and Greece. Greece possessed its own distinct and largely unified ethnic physiognomy right from the start of historical times, whereas Italy presents an intricate mosaic of racial and linguistic groups. For this reason, to study the beginnings of Greek history is indeed to study the origins of the Greek people, whereas in the Italian case we shall find ourselves obliged to pursue a series of separate investigations into the racial origins of the various groups – the Etruscans, the Latins, the Oscan-Umbrian speaking Italic peoples, the Apulians, the Veneti, the Ligurians and so forth (leaving aside the Greeks themselves and the Celts, whose origins are historically better attested). Nonetheless the problems themselves tend to be incorrectly posed, and their solution hindered, if these different investigations are too rigidly separated from each other (this applies particularly in the case of the origin of the Etruscans in relation to that of the peoples of Indo-European Italy). It is in fact becoming ever clearer that we must posit a whole range of mutual dependences between the elements that made up these peoples. This is borne out in the field of linguistics (for instance) by the existence of lexical commixtures and of certain common phonetic idiosyncrasies. Through a complex network of acts and events, this interdependence acquired fixed historical shape.

The beginnings of the history of the Italy of antiquity are not synonymous with the beginnings of its peoples. They do not amount simply or strictly to an ethno-genetic process, but involve aspects of social and political organisation, patterns of settlement and ways of life and forms of production, religious practices, mental habits, tastes and artistic traditions, and the like. All these may exist – and in fact prove to some extent to have existed – as the common property of different peoples, whatever their origins. The peoples in question, after all, developed and lived together from early times in the well-defined and somewhat restricted geographical milieu of the Italian region (especially in certain areas). The study of origins thus embraces not only the formation of the various separate historical nationalities, but all the variety of civilised life that flourished among them.

The formative elements: archaeological aspects

The Italy of antiquity would have been a quite different place without the precedent of the prehistoric centres of the Mezzogiorno – especially Apulia, Basilicata and Sicily. These ancient and highly developed centres endured for thousands of years, from the beginning of the neolithic period to the threshold of the Greek colonial era. It is worth emphasising, however, that the geographical area in question – whose archaeological exploration has been relatively recent and is still in progress – was to remain in the forefront of later developments, with the arrival of the Greek colonies themselves. It was the site where the great currents of civilising influence that crossed the sea from the Aegean and Anatolian world were received and diffused; it played its own role in the creative development of Mediterranean culture, producing artefacts whose technical and decorative sophistication matched that of their Oriental counterparts (for example, the neolithic painted pottery of the Serra d'Alto style). These were evidently stable and prosperous settlements. They evolved towards a truly proto-urban form (as at Coppa Nevigata in Apulia or the Castello di Lipari in the Aeolian islands), and had a developed economy of agricultural and artisanal production, with a well-marked social structure, considerable political organisation, and durable traditions and memories. Finally, almost the entire area participated in full in the great expansion of Mycenaean culture of the middle and late Bronze Age. All this must surely have had the most significant historical consequences.

It is rather harder to gain any vivid sense of the prehistoric lineaments of central and northern Italy. Here, the successive cultural phases were more on a level with those found elsewhere in Europe. Stable centres of population were no larger than villages, consisting of huts or cabins, or of pile-dwellings on lake- and river-shores; only towards the end of the Bronze Age did they become more numerous and densely populated, particularly in elevated situations. Stock-raising rather than agriculture predominated over large areas of the interior of the peninsula, where it was closely linked to the development and spread of the Apenninic civilisation of the Bronze Age. We have already noted the repeated influx of peoples and influences from continental Europe. These seem to be traceable above all to the Danube basin and the Balkans, more advanced in many respects than the Italian region (with the exception, of course, of the south); they indicate the existence of additional routes of communication across the Adriatic. The complex phenomena involved are already observable in the neolithic period, but they remain in evidence through the late Bronze Age and into the Iron Age, for we find styles and decorative modes in pottery, types of metal artefact, and so on. Less often apparent are influences from western Europe, such as the spread in the later neolithic of so-called 'bell-beakers' (found also in Sardinia and Sicily). We have some evidence of the religion, customs, costumes and figurative vocabulary of the inhabitants of primitive Italy in the more recent prehistoric period: the rock-drawings at Monte Bego in the maritime Alps and at Valcamonica in the central Alps, and the anthropomorphic stelae, or statues-*menhirs*, found in Corsica, the Lunigiana, the Alpine valleys and also in Apulia. The motifs found here undoubtedly draw on a more remote period of European prehistory, but they survived into the historical epoch, as we see in the funerary stelae of the Tuscan-Emilian and Apulian regions.

The advent and subsequent spread of cremation as a funeral rite is of considerable importance for its novelty, its extensive diffusion throughout Europe, the scope and significance that it later attained in Italy, and its intrinsic characteristics. It marked important stages in the historical development of the Italic world. It had its counterpart in the cultures of continental Europe known by the *Urnenfelder* or urnfields that they established. It penetrated into northern Italy in the late Bronze Age, being to some degree linked with the *terramare* culture; but it also appeared at more or less the same time in the south of the peninsula (a burial-ground at Canosa in Apulia seems to indicate its presence as early as the middle Bronze Age). Cremation attained its widest geographical diffusion in the Italian region in the last phase of the Bronze Age. The so-called 'proto-Villanovan' necropolises date from this time, among the most typical being those at Ascona in the canton of Ticino, at Fontanella Mantovana in Lombardy, at Bismantova in Emilia, in the Valle del Fiore and the Monti della Tolfa in Etruria, at Pianello di Genga in the Marches, at Timmari and Torre Castelluccia in Apulia, at Tropea in Calabria, and at Milazzo in Sicily. This phase, of which evidence exists also in the form of dwelling-places and metal repositories, was one of innovatory ferment and marked cultural development. In the Iron Age which followed, the rite of cremation faded, having established a lasting presence only in central Tyrrhenian Italy and in the north of the country. The problem of whether cremation was a practice peculiar, at least initially, to particular immigrant peoples who introduced it into Italy (and if so who those peoples were), whether it should rather be ascribed to the spread of certain religious ideas or cultural tastes, or whether – as is most probable – it derives from a combination of causes depending on time and circumstances, remains one of the great unanswered questions of Italian proto-history.

Archaeological data, clearly, can offer only external, mute and partial evidence of actual events – though this evidence is also immediate and authentic. From such data we can nonetheless gain an idea of the traditions and cultural trends which preceded and probably to some extent determined the forms taken by the civilisation of Italy in the historical period. We can also glean some valuable hints about conditions of life in prehistoric societies, their rise and fall, and the relations between them. Above all, we can establish a firm chronological framework. Uncertainties and controversies over points of detail aside, we can in fact place the facts and phenomena of the more recent era of Italian prehistory in sequence (relative chronology), and can even approximately date them (absolute chronology). The schema is as follows: neolithic era (from the sixth or fifth millennium BC (?) to the third millennium); the first metal working or late neolithic period and the early Bronze Age (from the third millennium to the first centuries of the second millennium); the middle Bronze Age, the period of the Apenninic civilisation and of the first Mycenaean influences (sixteenth to fourteenth centuries BC); the late Bronze Age, whose first phase saw the development of the sub-Apenninic civilisation and the height of Mycenaean influence (thirteenth–twelfth centuries) and whose final phase was marked by the spread of cremation and by proto-Villanovan cultural forms (end of twelfth century–beginning of ninth century); and finally the beginnings of Iron Age culture (ninth century onwards).

Within this framework and against this background of their

material life (everything that can be verified from material remains), we have to imagine all the largely hidden aspects of a prehistoric people's experience: the nature and activities of their group and community life, their contacts and conflicts, their migrations and interminglings, the formation or dissolution of ethnic nuclei, the way they thought, their beliefs and traditions, the spread of new ideas among them, and so forth. Material remains alone, however, are clearly an insufficient basis for the recreation of reality: they may prove positively misleading, and have often done so. We must also make use of the indirect and (so to speak) retrospective evidence obtainable from linguistic study, and from cautious critical scrutiny of literary tradition.

The advent and spread of Indo-European languages

The penetration of Italy by the Indo-European languages, a process of fundamental importance, must be considered in the long chronological perspective advocated above. It continued, however, into historical times (and may even be said to have been completed only with the achievement of Romanisation, by which Latin triumphed over the remnants of non-Indo-European speech, of which Etruscan was an important example). Thus it cannot be identified merely as a problem about origins – or, indeed, identified with 'the problem' of origins. It involved considerably broader perspectives, transcending the history not only of Italian antiquity but of antiquity itself.

So far as Italian prehistory is concerned, it seems beyond doubt that Indo-European languages were not originally spoken by the earliest inhabitants of the land of Italy, but were introduced from outside. It follows that they were preceded by other and different idioms, which linguists (as we have seen) call the 'substratum' or 'substrata'. We have already noted that our knowledge of these pre-Indo-European idioms depends essentially on the remnants or traces left in place-names and vocabulary: in consequence, it is very limited and uncertain, though this has not discouraged comparison with the substratum found in other, non-Italian areas of the Mediterranean and Europe. Scholars have even made some suggestions as to how these idioms should be grouped, and have spoken – though the issue is beset by doubt and controversy – of

Hispano-Caucasian (or Basque-Caucasian), of palaeo-European, Aegean-Asiatic, Rhaeto-Tyrrhenian, and so on. These idioms are thought to be linked to one another in both time and space. For instance, Hispano-Caucasian, belonging to the very remote past, seems to have survived in the Italian region only in the east and particularly in Sardinia, whereas the Aegean-Asiatic group is thought to have been among the most recent of the peninsular substrata, and perhaps even to have persisted after the first penetration of Indo-European languages. Typical examples of this idiom may include place-names in -*nt*-, such as Surrentum, or -s(s)a-, such as Temesa or Suessa, as well as certain lexical items referring to particular domains (especially the natural world) common to Greek and Latin, which may have passed from the substratum into both Greek and Latin: for instance, *leirion: lilium* and *sukon: ficus*. Archaeological evidence shows that there were lively cultural contacts during the neolithic and Bronze Ages between Italy and the eastern Mediterranean: some have even spoken of prehistoric 'colonisations' of the Italian coastal region and Sicily. We shall see that the problem of the origin of the Etruscan language should itself perhaps be seen in this context.

Given this non-Indo-European ethnic and linguistic foundation, rooted in the remote prehistoric past, we must now ask how and when the Indo-European languages, whose imprint is so clearly seen in the ethnography of Italy in historical times, were first introduced. If, as is now believed, the Indo-European language group was originally spoken by peoples living between eastern Europe and the borderlands of central Asia, this speech-type must have made its way to Italy from the Danube basin and the Balkans. As we have seen, archaeological evidence from the prehistoric period does show the impact of influences from that area from the neolithic onwards. It is quite certain that the spread of the language was initiated by actual migrations of groups of people who were its 'bearers'. We can assume that these same groups also introduced some cultural innovations. But we know nothing about the details of these transmission processes – the paths they followed, their circumstances, sequence and extent. We know only that these movements from north-east to south-west took place by way of an overland route through the eastern Alps and – to much greater effect – by the sea route across the Adriatic. The continental advance of Indo-European culture presents a picture of large-scale pressures and upheavals. This is the context in which we can place the migrations of tribal and ethnic groups, and indeed of small isolated communities, into Italy. These may have consisted of a gradual spread or – why not? – of sudden conquests and expeditions; but the whole process took place over a great length of time, in a gradual but irresistible progression. The wide diffusion of Indo-European speech in Italy at the dawn of the historical era, and the degree to which these languages had evolved internally (both in the inter-relation of different Indo-European idioms and in their interaction with the linguistic substrata), demonstrate incontrovertibly that their advent in Italy must predate the earliest written documents by very many centuries. It must have occurred far back in prehistory, before the Bronze Age – as early as the late neolithic or even the neolithic. On the other hand, the process can be said to have continued beyond the threshold of historical times if we include as part of its last phase the introduction of the Indo-European dialects of the Celts into the plains of the Po valley. Indeed the Greek colonisations can also be seen as one aspect of the spread of Indo-European culture into Italy.

Let us now look at the character and distribution of the various individual Indo-European language-types for whose existence in Italy there is historical evidence. We have already noted that the great historically attested languages – Latin, Oscan-Umbrian, Messapian – developed slowly. This long process must have involved a convergence of linguistic currents. Some of these must have vanished; there must have been mutual interaction; elements of the pre-Indo-European substrata must have played a part. Still, we can discern certain structural features that allow us to place the process, tentatively, within the wider framework of relations between the various linguistic groups of the western Indo-European area. For instance, scholars now tend to agree about the marginal and archaic features of Latin; the more 'central' and developed characteristics of Oscan-Umbrian (which may give it some kinship with Breton and Greek); the relationship of Venetic to Latin and German; and the parallels which Messapian displays, linguistically and in personal nomenclature, with the speech of an area of the Balkans identified historically as Thrace in the east and Illyria (including modern Albania) in the west. The distribution of the languages known to history corresponds significantly with this suggested framework. Latin indeed appears in Tyrrhenian Italy as an outpost of Indo-European, perhaps representing a first and particularly early surge to the west under the pressure of other innovatory impulses. This earliest layer in the peninsular area is matched, in the north, by the establishment of Venetic, involving some degree of transalpine communication. The fanning out of the Oscan-Umbrian or eastern Italic group of dialects from the middle Adriatic area into central and southern Italy may be understood as a second and later wave of Indo-European influence affecting Italy, while the Messapian tongue of Apulia (the clearest case, whose traces are still visible) reveals its kinship with the Illyrian spoken on the opposite shore of the sea.

Against the overall background summed up here, we may suggest – as hypotheses – some more detailed features of the spread of Indo-European into Italy. The earliest centres of linguistic innovation may well have been the flourishing pre-historic settlements of south-east Italy. Once established here, new forms would have spread, influencing the rest of the peninsula. Such a hypothesis undeniably tends to reverse the traditional view that the first Indo-European speakers made their way from north to south. The thesis of penetration from the south applies, however, only to the earliest of the waves mentioned in the previous paragraph. This may have culminated in the establish-ment of Latin, and must also have involved other dialects that have vanished or that existed only in isolation (as seems to have been the case with the dialect of the historically known Sicels). This is the stratum which F. Ribezzo called 'Ausonian' and G. Devoto 'proto-Latin', and which might better be known as 'western Italic'. Even these first currents of Indo-European linguistic influence may in fact have flowed into Italy by way of the Adriatic coast and by land from the north (Venetic has seemed to some to be a case in point). This sea route across the Adriatic was in all probability the path taken by the second great linguistic wave, identified with Oscan-Umbrian or 'eastern Italic' (or, as some call it, simply 'Italic'). We shall see that this was still actively spreading westwards towards the Tyrrhenian coast and southern Italy during the historical era. Finally, the influence of Illyrian on Apulia, from which Messapian derives, can be dated to the final phase of prehistory, probably to the Bronze Age.

Last but not least, it seems to me worth emphasising that, while the advent of Indo-European languages in Italy certainly implies the arrival of new peoples, we would undoubtedly be mistaken to think that this entailed any general submergence or annihilation of the previous inhabitants, or even that it changed them very profoundly. This is shown by the general continuity of prehistoric cultures and settlements, and also more specifically, within the sphere of linguistic change itself, by the marked traces left on the newly superimposed tongues by the substrata. We have already referred to these. They are particularly evident in the fact that the historical Indo-European languages (especially Latin) have assimilated into their vocabulary a large number of pre-Indo-European terms. This points to a long period of cohabitation and a gradual fusion between local communities and immigrant groups. Moreover, even those parts of Italy never fully Indo-Europeanised – these progressively shrank with the advance of Indo-European culture, and at the dawn of the historical era perhaps consisted of the Tuscan-Ligurian region and the islands, excluding eastern Sicily – were probably subject to Indo-European influence. Sometimes, as in the case of the Etruscan language, this influence may have been profound.

Heroic tradition and the evidence for a historical view of the late Bronze Age

If we are to give the data reviewed thus far some concrete historical substance, and an element of what we might call 'human interest', we can turn, duly armed with caution and reservations, to the accounts found in classical literary tradition, insofar as these deal with the times and places we are discussing. The credibility of these sources might seem to be nullified by their remoteness in time from the deeds which they narrate, by their essentially mythical character, and by the arbitrary – if learned – nature of the inferences drawn from them by the historians and ethnographers of antiquity. Modern critical scholarship, however, appears increasingly inclined to accept that the legends may contain echoes of actual events, memory of which may also have been orally transmitted to classical Greek historiographers and ethnographers. What is now widely accepted for the proto-history of the second millennium BC in Greece should surely not be rejected when we turn to the contemporaneous proto-history of Italy, especially when we bear in mind the mutual dependence of the two areas.

Evidence of this kind may improve our understanding of the landfalls made on the Italian coast by individual sailors or by groups, and the relations that developed between them and the local population. We have mentioned the repeated accounts of how heroic strangers establish their predominance through displays of valour, win the fealty of local kings, marry their daughters, gain prestige and prerogatives, conquer lands, and found cities. This is a romantic version of historical and ethnological reality – of what happens when people from across the sea, with their own language and traditions, land and establish a permanent presence. Moreover, the traditional tales also refer to the established population of Italy and to movements of peoples within it, and these references afford an equally valuable source of historically useful information. The material is scattered amongst numerous surviving Greek and Latin literary sources. Even more important writings were doubtless contained in some of the documents that have perished, especially the work of the Sicilian Greek historical school (Antiochus, Philistus, Timaeus of Taormina). Dionysus of Halicarnassus, the historian who wrote during the Augustan period, gives a useful chronology of the legendary materials in the first book of his *Roman Antiquities*.

The earliest records concern the overseas migrations of the Arcadians and their arrival in southern Italy some seventeen generations before the Trojan War (which implies a date, in modern terms, around the eighteenth or seventeenth century BC), and the spread of their descendants throughout the extremity of the peninsula, both towards the Tyrrhenian coast and Sicily and towards the central areas of the Apennines. These immigrants were called the Oenotrians, after their mythical king and leader, Oenotrius (this name of Oenotrians or *Oinotroi*, cognate with the Greek *oinos*, wine, is probably fictitious, as are their supposed Greek Arcadian origins). The territory they occupied was known as Oenotria, and was so extensive that this name became a synonym for Italy. The Oenotrians were linked, in a complex web of identity and succession, with the peoples known as the Chones, the Italici, the Morgetes, the Sicels and the Ausonians (corresponding to the mythical kings Italus, Morgetis, Siculus and Auson). These peoples were regarded as having populated a large part of southern Italy and Sicily. A branch of the Oenotrians which had made its way northwards was held to be the ancestral stock of the Aborigines, and through them of the Latins. Fabulous though these narratives may be, their tale of the penetration of Italy by the Oenotrians in ancient times is undeniably consistent, chronologically, with the fact that Balkan and Aegean culture exerted marked cultural influence during the early Bronze Age in Italy. Above all, it is remarkable that the account tallies in the sphere of linguistics with what we know concerning the advent and diffusion of the earliest wave of Indo-European influence (discussed above) – what has been called the Ausonian or proto-Latin phase.

The traditional narrative gains further richness and interest when we come to the account of how the Ausonians were driven out of Apulia and pushed westwards by the immigration of the Iapygians, who came from across the Adriatic. From this we can infer, first of all, that the original territory of the Ausonians stretched from the extreme south-east of Italy to Campania (where they are known to history as neighbours of the Opici), into Latium, where they appear under the Latinised name of Aurunci, and as far as the Aeolian islands, conquered by Liparus, son of Auson. This amounts to virtually the entire area elsewhere attributed to the Oenotrians (and Ausonia, like Oenotria, was a name used to denote Italy). Secondly, this corroborates the hypothesis of racial movements from east to west: these groups were eclipsed in the eastern areas, and displaced by the arrival of the Messapian-speaking Iapygians, and their descendants flourished in the west in the tribes of the Latins and probably also the Sicels. We also see movement from east to west in the migratory travels of Liparus, son of king Auson, and Aeolus, who left southern Italy for the Aeolian islands: from here, their descendants are said to have gained dominion over part of Sicily and of modern Calabria, founding dynasties that endured until the dawn of the historical era. Also noteworthy is the very vivid account of the journey made by the Sicels from the peninsula to Sicily. Thucydides (VI, 2) places this three centuries before the historically verifiable colonisations of the Greeks, or in other words around the eleventh century BC. Archaeological investigation has in fact brought to light quite marked evidence, from the period around the end of the second millennium, of features of the culture of peninsular Italy both in the Aeolian islands, where scholars actually speak of 'Ausonian' cultures, and in eastern Sicily. Further confirmation is provided by linguistic study which has established the affinity of the Sicel language, spoken in the eastern part of the island, with the Italic languages and in particular, it would seem, with Latin.

Numerous accounts refer to contacts between the Aegean and Italian worlds after this first Arcadian immigration. These are said to have occurred just before, during or after the Trojan War, which took place, according to the most reliable traditional computations, around the end of the thirteenth and the beginning of the twelfth centuries. The traditional stories provide settings in Italy, and in particular along the Tyrrhenian coastline, for such myths as those of Heracles or of the Argonauts; they show Daedalus' Sicilian and Sardinian exploits, chronicle the Sardinian adventures of Aristaeus, Iolaus and the Thespians, and so on. All this goes to show the importance of the land and seas of Italy in the development of the Greek myths. Such narratives apart, a number of individual legends may have some value as traces of the underlying historical scenario of the period we are concerned with. Of particular interest are the accounts of the Sicilian expedition of Minos, king of Crete. Minos is said to have visited the court of king Cocalus, in the city of Camicus in the territory of the Sicani, and to have been killed there through an act of treachery. Following this, we are told, the indigenous inhabitants defeated the Cretans in battle, and expelled most of them from the island. In the course of these events, the city of Minoa is said to have been founded, not far from the future site of Agrigento (Akragas). Certain details of the archaeological finds made near S. Angelo Muxaro, which is thought to be in the same area as the Camicus of antiquity, and more generally the widespread occurrence in Sicily of features derived from the Aegean (such as excavated tombs in the form of a *tholos* or pseudo-cupola, and so on), give considerable probability to this story. It has a wealth of detail and may well relate an episode illustrating the extent to which Crete remained a maritime power even after its conquest by the Achaeans. Tradition also records that the Cretans were present in Apulia. However, the legends mainly focus on the heroes of the Trojan War: Greeks such as Ulysses, Diomedes and Philoctetes, the companions of Nestor in his homeward voyage (*nostoi*), or Trojans such as Aeneas and Antenor. Each of these personages, interestingly, has his own more or less precisely localised centre of memorials and cults: Ulysses in the Tyrrhenian sea, Diomedes in the Adriatic, Philoctetes and the companions of Nestor in southern Italy, Aeneas in Latium, Antenor in the Venetian region. Another series of narratives tells of the arrival in Italy of the Pelasgians from the Aegean, and of the Lydians under their captain Tyrrhenus, son of king Atys, known more generically as the Tyrrhenians (*Tyrsenoi*) who are identified with the Etruscans. This accumulation of stories, various and fantastic as they are, must clearly be founded (as their concentration in a fairly brief time-span would suggest) in an actual phase of heightened contact between Italy and the Aegean world. This was in the middle and especially the later Bronze Age, as is attested by the abundance and wide geographical distribution of Mycenaean imported artefacts and influences (which are, moreover, particularly in evidence in those parts of southern Italy and Sicily most prominent in the legendary record).

In historical terms, then, we can suggest that there was a period when the Aegean presence in the Italian region (reflected in the traditional accounts and confirmed by archaeological evidence) perhaps reached the point where truly colonial or 'pre-colonial' Mycenaean settlements were established – at Lo Scoglio del Tonno near Taranto, at Thapsos in Sicily, and possibly in the Aeolian islands and at Vivara and Ischia in the Gulf of Naples. Progressive trends affected Italy and transformed the indigenous societies, already deeply affected and altered by Indo-European influence. This period was crucially important in initiating the process that ultimately created the historical structures of classical Italy. Legendary records of the successive reigns of Oenotrius, Italus, Morgetis and Siculus (perhaps reflected in the writings of the historian Antiochus of Syracuse) may reflect the actual existence in early times of extensive state organisations. These may have been based on the Mycenaean model even after the collapse of the Mycenaean political and economic order. Something similar may hold in the case of the empire of Aeolus, subdivided into the kingdoms of his sons Jocastus (situated in modern Calabria), Pheraimon, Androcles, Xuthos, Agathyrnos (occupying various parts of Sicily), and Asyochos (in Lipari). We need not regard such accounts as complete inventions. In Sicily, we see alongside the well-established Mycenaean traditions of the eastern coast an influx of 'Ausonian' innovations from the Aeolian islands. Moreover, as we have noted, all the late Bronze Age cultures, including those of the peninsula, show innovating tendencies. We may well feel that we are witnessing the emergence of a historical civilisation when we contemplate (to take two major 'proto-Villanovan' complexes) the royal or sacred edifice of Luni sul Mignone, in southern Etruria, or the great river-port of Frattesina in the Po delta.

At this point, we must mention a controversial problem concerning the relations between Italy and the eastern Mediterranean in the late Bronze Age, namely the eastern origins of the so-called 'peoples of the sea'. These peoples are recorded as attacking Egypt between the late thirteenth and early twelfth centuries BC (then under the pharaohs Meneptah and Rameses III), and also mentioned as mercenaries in the Egyptian army. They include, as well as some peoples whose origin we can confidently ascribe to the Aegean and Anatolian world (among them the Achaeans themselves and the *Plst*, that is the Philistians, who may perhaps be identified with the Pelasgians), peoples bearing the names *Trš (Turša)*, *Šrdn (Šardana* or *Šerdani)* and *Šklš (Šakalaša)*. Since the last century, some scholars have sought to identify these respectively with the Tyrrhenians *(Tyrsenói)*, the Sardinians *(Sardanioi)* and the Sicels *(Sikelói)*. These name-correspondences are certainly tempting (and in the case of the *Šrdn* there are also similarities with the costumes worn by Sardinian warriors in bronze figurines). But it remains uncertain whether we are dealing here with tribes that migrated into the eastern Mediterranean and subsequently found their way into the Italian region (which would confirm the Greek legendary accounts in their attribution of an overseas origin to the ancestors of some of the Italic peoples), or with tribes already settled in the Italian islands and peninsula who may have taken part – perhaps as allies or mercenaries fighting with the Achaeans, or in some other way –in the wars and upheavals which concluded the Mycenaean age in the eastern Mediterranean. In the latter case documents written at the time would in a sense confirm that late Bronze Age Italy was beginning to acquire historical identity.

The birth of historical Italy

It is undoubtedly to the Iron Age, or in other words to the eighth and ninth centuries BC, that we must turn for the first stages in the process of differentiation, stabilisation and further development that formed the great ethnic units of historical Italy, which remained substantially unchanged until unification under Rome. Archaeological discoveries are especially eloquent in this regard. In earlier periods, material remains furnish little useful ethnological evidence. Only with difficulty can we discern some relation between cultural features and the linguistic changes that accompanied or followed Indo-Europeanisation, for the cultural evidence of the Apenninic Bronze Age on the Italian peninsula is spread over a wide area and shows very little differentiation between one territory and another. As we approach the end of the Bronze Age, however, around 1000 BC, certain local peculiarities appear, despite the substantially uniform character of what has come down to us from the 'proto-Villanovan' phase; and these local peculiarities anticipate the well-marked cultural boundaries of the Iron Age. In Apulia, for instance, the period typified by the painted pottery usually called 'proto-Iapygian' undoubtedly reveals the presence of immigrants from Illyria, who introduced the Messapian tongue and are to be identified with the Iapygians of historical record. And in Latium, we see the emergence of a typical culture using cremating rites and hut-urns, the so-called proto-Latial culture. This merges without a break into the culture of Iron-Age Latium, whose authors are quite certainly the Latini.

In the Iron Age, cultural regions become clearly perceptible in which we can recognise the 'national' groupings of the Italic world. They correspond more or less exactly with the linguistic areas evident in the inscriptions of immediately succeeding centuries and to the territories of the historical peoples recorded in literary sources. In most cases, the correspondence is quite obvious, as is shown by a comparison between the outline distribution-maps depicting the cultural areas of the Iron Age and the languages of classical Italy (see figures 1 and 2). Here – within the given limits of time, place and circumstance – it must be conceded that 'Kossinna's law' appears to hold good. In other cases, the correspondence is less certain or more nebulous, partly owing to the incompleteness of our knowledge and partly, no doubt, because the ethnic groupings themselves were in an embryonic and unstable state even in historical times, as was the case in some areas of central Italy and above all in the plain of the Po and in the

Alpine region. Besides, no archaeological 'test', obviously, can disclose the multiform and complex reality of the historical movement which led from the Italy of prehistory to the formation of stable territorial entities, with their own habits of speech, traditions and customs. From this there arose a consciousness that such entities existed, as the nations (the Latin technical term was *nomina*, 'names') of historical Italy. The process is largely beyond our knowledge. It may have been determined at various times by the power of particular individuals or groups, by defeat or conquest, by the common development of productive activity, by the emergence of interests focused on sanctuaries, markets, centres of settlement, and so on. The key point is that the basic ethnic structures of the Italy of antiquity were established through the beginning of the first millennium BC, in the historical and cultural environment of the early Iron Age. That new age, over and above the particular developments it involved, must undoubtedly have taken shape through the impact of commonly felt stimuli, and have shown a high degree of interdependence: an indication that the framework of Italic history had a certain unity right from the beginning.

In our unravelling of this web of formative and stabilising processes, we shall begin from the south, following a line at once geographical and chronological. The south was in the van of events from prehistoric times. Southern Italy and Sicily, as we have said, perhaps reached what we might call a historical level of complexity (proto-urban settlements, state-like politics, and so on) as early as the late Bronze Age – possibly as a result of its exposure to the cultural influence of Mycenae. As to its actual structure, we can only put forward hypotheses, interpreting the legends about the kingdoms of the Oenotrians, Ausonians, Sicels and Aeolians along with such data as archaeology affords. This 'palaeo-Italic' phase, if indeed it occurred, must however have passed its zenith by the time the Greek colonists arrived in the eighth century BC. Greek colonisation probably helped to block or divert its further autonomous development. Its last remnants must have been absorbed by the Iapygians, who pressed in from the east, and above all by the eastern Italic peoples of Oscan-Umbrian speech, who came down from the north. This explains why what may have been the opening chapter of Italic history was soon lost in oblivion. No really lasting national entity emerged from these tribes. Oenotrians, Ausonians, Italici, Morgetes, Sicels – the very names

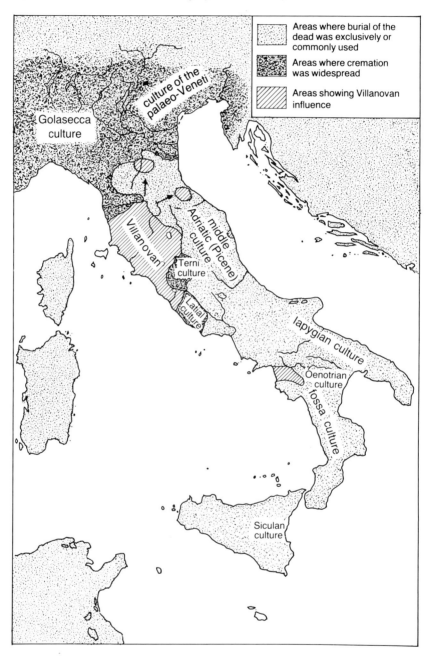

Figure 1   Cultural areas of Italy at the beginning of the Iron
Age (ninth century BC).

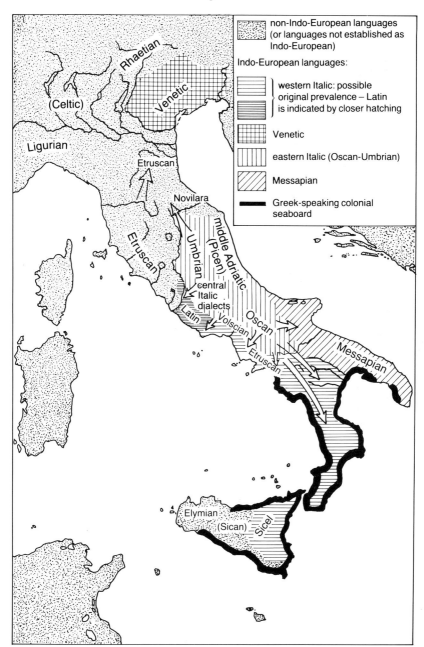

Figure 2 Original distribution and spread of the languages of earliest Italy.

(where they are not different terms for a single stock) mostly remain wrapped in a mist of legend. If they are used in later times, they almost always refer to the past (though as we shall see the very vigorous Sicels of Sicily proved an exception to this rule). Archaeological traces of the Iron Age are also abundant in the relevant areas, namely (Sicily apart), in modern Calabria, Basilicata and Campania, where the so-called *Fossa* culture flourished and where densely populated and long-inhabited settlements upriver from the Greek colonies have been discovered (above all in Basilicata) with painted geometric pottery of characteristically 'Oenotrian' type. The very name *Italia*, Italy, is derived from the Itali settled in what is today Calabria: the Greeks gradually came to use it as a designation for the entire peninsular Mezzogiorno, though only much later, at the time of the Roman conquests, was the term extended to cover the whole of the peninsula and eventually the Alpine region too.

Apulia (known as Puglia in modern Italy, but in English generally still called Apulia) was the original territory of the Ausonians and Oenotrians. Under Illyrian influence during the Bronze Age, it developed its own distinctive civilisation from the Iron Age onwards. This was the creation of the Iapygians (or Apuli, which is the Latin version of Iapygi), who can be subdivided into the Messapians in the south, the Peucetians in the centre, and the Daunians in the north. These peoples soon developed urban-sized centres of population. Their products included painted geometric vases of great refinement, which varied from one locality to the next, as well as funerary *stelae* in the region occupied by the Daunians. These resembled the human form and bore bas-relief engravings, both figurative and ornamental. Although it must have been in communication with other cultural areas of the south, Apulia gives the impression of heightened specialisation and of a certain isolation, due perhaps to the nature of the recently settled immigrant tribes themselves. This isolation is perceptible from the outset, and – as we shall see – it was to have significant historical consequences.

The inhabitants of Campania and Latium may have been distantly related, ethnically, to the 'palaeo-Italic' peoples of the Mezzogiorno. Campania (using the term in its widest, modern sense) had no clear cultural or (presumably) ethnic-cultural profile in the Iron Age. Much of the region was in the area of the *Fossa* culture, probably attributable to the Ausonians and Opici. In the territory of the modern province of Salerno, however, and particularly at Pontecagnano on the coastal plain and at Sala Consilina in the Tanagro valley, cremation burial-grounds have been discovered markedly similar to those of the Villanovan Iron-Age civilisation of Etruria. This suggests that very early Etruscan influence (of a colonial or 'pre-colonial' type?) may already have been felt here in the ninth century BC. The Greeks may well also have reached the Gulf of Naples at a very early date (during the first half of the eighth century). If we bear in mind that eastern Italic peoples, too, may have come down from the mountainous interior, though without leaving visible traces, then we can understand why the primitive inhabitants of Campania never established a distinctive community. Beyond the 'zone of silence' of southern Latium, north of the Monti Ausoni, in the area subsequently known as *Latium vetus* ('old Latium'), the picture is quite different. Here, as we have already noted, a civilisation emerged in the late Bronze Age and at the opening of the Iron Age – during the tenth and ninth centuries – which used cremation rites and hut-like cinerary urns. This was centred especially in the Alban Mountains, but was present also in the area where Rome was coming into being. This first phase of Latin life was followed by a period in which inhumation was the favoured form of burial and which may well have been influenced by the *Fossa* culture of the south. At this time, in the course of the eighth and seventh centuries, many of the original modest villages rose to the status of proto-urban settlements. A few, such as Rome, were becoming cities in the full sense. Greek influence was spreading, as was an orientalising civilisation borrowed, beyond a shadow of a doubt, from the Etruscans. The eastern Italic peoples, or Sabines, were pressing down from the interior, and the political-economic supremacy of the Etruscans was establishing itself more or less everywhere in the region.

And so we come to the Etruscans, without whom it would be impossible to picture the history of the Italy of antiquity either in its origins or subsequently. Modern scholars, as is well known, disagree about the origins of the Etruscans. They have often been regarded as immigrants from overseas, from the east. This matches the classical tradition that the Tyrrhenians (as the Greeks called the Etruscans) were descended from the Lydians, or identical to the

Pelasgians, or were at any rate migrants of some kind into Italy from the Aegean, in particular from the island of Lemnos. (On Lemnos, there is an inscription in a pre-Hellenic tongue that offers the closest known parallel to the Etruscan language.) Other experts ascribe to them a northern origin, parallel or subsequent to that of the 'Italici'. Still others follow the celebrated classical theory of Dionysus of Halicarnassus and see the Etruscans as indigenous inhabitants, descended from the pre-Indo-European population of Italy. Most of the theories reveal a rather obvious tendency to isolate the problem of the origins of the Etruscans from that of the origins of Italic peoples generally: this, clearly, because Etruscan is basically a non-Indo-European language. However, simplistic formulae cannot resolve the issue. The various arguments advanced are compatible, not conflicting, so long as we understand the birth of Etruscan nationality and civilisation in sufficiently broad chronological terms – as a process of formation going back well before the onset of the historical era – just as we must do for the other races of the Italic world. This implies an inevitable interaction and cross-fertilisation with the origins of the other peoples. We have already drawn attention to the overall relation between the cultural areas of the Iron Age and the ethno-linguistic demarcations of historical Italy. Within this framework there is a clear correspondence between the culture known as 'Villanovan' (after Villanova, near Bologna, where it was first discovered: it is typified especially by the use of cremation and biconic cinerary urns) and the territory inhabited by the Etruscans in fully historical times, namely not only Etruria proper but also part of Emilia, Romagna and Campania. In our view, there can no longer be any doubt that Villanovan culture marks the earliest expression of the civilisation of the already established Etruscan people. Their origins, accordingly, must be sought in earlier times — during the Bronze Age, at a time corresponding to the Etrurian 'proto-Villanovan' culture (highly developed, as we know), or still further in the past. The linguistic data suggest that they may have developed in an area relatively immune to Indo-European innovations, and that they may have been much affected by Aegean influence (perhaps reflected in the legendary accounts of the migrations of the Pelasgians and Tyrrhenians). The presence of Villanovan features in northern and Adriatic Italy (there is a small area recognised as Villanovan at Fermo in the Marches) and in the south demonstrates that the Etruscans were already enjoying a phase of expansion as early as the ninth century. Their influence may have encouraged the peoples whom it affected to develop their own identities. In Etruria itself, Villanovan culture underwent rapid and intensive growth during the eighth century: villages were transformed into proto-urban centres, and the way was opened for the eastern influences that gave rise to the orientalising civilisation of the seventh century.

Also prominent in the emerging ethnic-cultural landscape of classical Italy were the many and various peoples who spoke Oscan-Umbrian dialects – in other words, the eastern Italic peoples. In the historical era, we find them scattered over a wide territory, which includes the centre of the peninsula and the Adriatic coast, and actively expanding towards the Tyrrhenian Sea and the Ionian Sea and north towards Romagna. They appear with different characteristics, and at different times, in different places. Nonetheless, especially in the light of the latest discoveries and studies, we can speak of a distinctive ethnic entity that can be given the general name of Sabines (or, in their own phonology, *Safini*) which came into being no later than the early Iron Age in an area including parts of the Marches and the Abruzzi and the province of Rieti. The earliest significant cultural expression of this people is the civilisation commonly known as 'Picenian' (from the name Piceni or Picenti given to one of the branches of the original stock). This flourished in the Marches and the northern Abruzzi, and was heavily affected by Adriatic influences. However, the presence of the Sabines, and evidence of their westward movement, can be discerned as far afield as the Tiber valley – and in quite early times, moreover, for they were traditionally held to have played a part in the foundation of Rome itself. Other peoples belonging to the same original nucleus, whose differentiation into separate groupings probably came about rather later, include the various inhabitants of the Abruzzi (Vestini, Marsi, Peligni, Marrucini and so forth), while among their counterparts to the south we can number the Samnites of Molise and Campania. These latter gave rise, when they spread in the historical period, to the Campanians, Lucanians and Bruttii. It is probable, though detailed evidence is hard to come by, that the eastern Italic peoples began to move northwards during this same original phase, establishing themselves in Umbria and subsequently in Romagna.

It is remarkable that the 'Picenian' civilisation of the Adriatic coast should have extended as far as the Pesaro area, where inscriptions discovered in the Novilara necropolis have proved to be in a language difficult to classify and unlike that spoken by the eastern Italic peoples. This shows how the process of ethnic consolidation left traces here and there of primitive groups who resisted its amalgamating tendency. This was especially true around the edges of the extensive area of the eastern Po plain (comprising modern Emilia, Romagna and parts of Lombardy and the Veneto). Here, the expansion of the Etruscan, Venetic and Umbrian peoples must have taken place against a background of earlier, still surviving settlement by non-Indo-European or pioneering Indo-European inhabitants – such as the Euganei, who are no more than a name to us now.

In the Veneto, there emerged a very well-defined set of ethnic-cultural features, among the most clearly marked in all the regions of pre-Roman Italy. Here, the local 'proto-Villanovan' culture gave birth at the beginning of the Iron Age (in the ninth and eighth centuries bc) to the civilisation that we know as 'palaeo-Venetian' or 'Atestine' (the latter term is derived from Ateste, the Roman name of Este, an especially rich source of relevant archaeological finds). The surprising longevity of its features, which endure well into the historical era, indicate that this culture was an early expression of the ethnic identity of the Veneti, who settled in the area between the Alps, Istria and the river Adige. Cremation was their usual burial-custom, and their artefacts included embossed articles in laminated bronze typical of the so-called 'situla culture'. Relatively isolated though it was, this world shows signs of contact with the Villanovan culture of Emilia and with Picenian civilisation, as well as with the Iron Age cultures of central Europe (Hallstatt) and Slovenia.

We have still to consider the whole vast area of the central and western Po plain and the Alps. Here, the question of origins must be approached almost entirely on the basis of archaeological evidence, for linguistic and historical data relating to clearly defined national groups, where they exist at all, are of doubtful value and refer only to rather recent times. We are familiar with the names of many tribes and peoples. In terms of the most general classification, we know that the central and eastern Alps were inhabited by the Rhaetians, and that the Ligurians occupied a large part of north-western Italy, as well as some areas beyond the Alps; while the subsequent advent of the Celts affected the whole future of these areas. But the overall framework eludes us. We are unable to draw exact territorial or chronological frontiers. Here, we feel the process of ethnic definition was still actively evolving in the historical era, as it had been elsewhere in Italy in prehistoric times. It is thus difficult to establish when and how the Celts spread through the region, though it is clear that their advance was nomadic rather than systematic (as we shall see when we return to them in Chapter 4), and that they mingled with the pre-existing inhabitants of Liguria and other races. The Lepontians, based around the lakes of Lombardy, were certainly Celts or forerunners of the Celts. Archaeologically, we can discern a fairly well-marked cultural area, lying mostly in Lombardy, which had been established by the Iron Age: it is referred to as the 'Golasecca civilisation', and predominantly practised cremation. It had precursors in the late Bronze Age, but cannot confidently be identified with any known ethnic grouping.

The final and in some respects conclusive phase in the establishment of the historical framework of the Italy of antiquity came with the founding of the Greek colonies. Although the process of ethnic differentiation was well advanced by this time (the early eighth century BC), colonisation hastened and shaped the development of the Italic communities. It gave them stimuli which to a varying extent shaped their own eventual character: the model of the city, the notion of public rights and laws, writing, monumental architecture, splendid figurative art, and other aspects of advanced civilisation. This brought to a close a cycle of progress, development and differentiation that had begun some centuries earlier with the impulse given by the Mycenaeans. This cycle encompasses the first phase of the history, or (as some would have it) the proto-history, of the Italic world.

3

The Flowering of Italy
in the Archaic Period
(Eighth to Fifth Centuries BC)

The Flowering of Italy
in the Archaic Period
(Eighth to Fifth Centuries BC)

Greek colonisation

It is impossible to imagine how the history and civilisation of Italy
in antiquity might have developed had the Greeks not founded
colonies in the Mezzogiorno and Sicily. Colonisation was a
phenomenon of the first importance, whose direct or indirect
influence permeated most of the territory and population of Italy.
Its beginnings in the eighth century marked the full entry of Italy
into the historical era, coinciding as they did with the establishment of the major ethnic-cultural groupings and the first movements towards urban living. This trend towards the creation of
cities is indeed one aspect of the developing dialectical relationship
between the culture of the local peoples and that of the immigrants
(not only colonists, but also merchants, sailors and craftsmen):
other aspects include the spread of alphabetic writing, coming
from Euboea, or – on a less profound plane – the importation and
copying of geometrical painted pottery. The indigenous national
traditions, conditioned by the same overall forces, expressed
themselves in differentiated forms as can be seen in the typical
example of the Etruscan and Latin alphabets, derived from the
Euboean originals of Pithecusae and Cumae respectively. Coastal
navigation, which flourished from the Ionian Sea to the Tyrrhenian
Sea, brought trade in techniques, images and ideas as well as in
commodities. The mineral-rich areas of Populonia and Vetulonia,
which contained some of the richest metal deposits then being
worked in the Mediterranean world, attracted those in search of
raw materials from Greece and from the Orient. As C. F. C.
Hawkes rightly noted, this played a part in shaping certain
prominent features of Etruria's historical character – its apparent
openness to exotic influences and its cultural eclecticism, its

tendency towards the creation of industrial-artisan and mercantile society, and its relative adaptability and tolerance of change in legal and intellectual ideas.

Nonetheless, we face grave problems when we attempt to draw historical conclusions from such evidence as is available. For the earliest phase, at least, of the intercourse of Greeks and non-Greeks in Italy, archaeological testimony is miscellaneous, fragmentary and equivocal, while the literary sources are few and date from after the period in question. We are faced with gaps and uncertainties, some of them bearing on fundamental points, and any attempted reconstruction of events must therefore be extremely hypothetical, approximate and provisional. New discoveries may at any moment alter or transform the picture. The materials are still being gathered. This was illustrated, for example, on the island of Ischia, where finds made during the excavation of the necropolis and settlement at Pithecusae, dating back to the first half of the eighth century, proved to have revolutionary implications for our understanding of the very earliest Greek colonies and of their relations with the indigenous cultures of central Italy. Results of similar importance have been obtained from recent and current explorations in Sicily, present-day Calabria, Campania and Latium.

Modern historical scholarship can be confident as to the main outlines, at least, of the great process of Greek settlement along the coasts of southern Italy and Sicily, for here classical literature offers a wealth of information, even though this is somewhat scattered. In particular, we can turn to Herodotus, Thucydides, Diodorus Siculus and Strabo – though the earliest historical account of the Greek colonies, in the works of Antiochus and Philistus of Syracuse, Timaeus of Taormina, and others, has unfortunately been lost, and has come down to us only in echoes and fragments. There is, besides, a great abundance of evidence in the fields of topography and monumental architecture, archaeology and inscriptions, and this grows continually with the progress of modern field research, conducted on an unprecedented scale in recent decades.

Exploratory or commercial voyages may have been undertaken before any colonies properly so called were founded (hence the disputed term, and concept, of 'pre-colonisation'). But leaving these aside, it would seem that the earliest known, or at any rate recognisable, attempts at colonisation of Italian territory were undertaken from the island of Euboea, or in other words from the two Ionian city-states of Chalcis and Eretria, first in conjunction and subsequently from the former only. These early ventures took settlers as far afield as the Tyrrhenian area, the furthest limit ever reached by Greek colonisation. They gave birth, during the second and third quarters of the eighth century, first of all to the remote outpost of Pithecusae facing the coast of Campania, then shortly afterwards to the mainland site at Cumae, and thence to the first settlements at Zancle on the Straits of Messina and at Naxos on the eastern coast of Sicily. There then followed a series of settlements, arising from the interplay of various groups and factors (including some not related to Euboean influence). These waxed and waned in strength. They included the firm foundation of Zancle-Messina and the forerunners of Reggio, Leontinoi and Catania. It is not impossible that settlers from Rhodes played some part in these earliest colonial ventures, for apart from its other activities in the western seas Rhodes was credited with the half-legendary foundation of Parthenope.

At all events, immigrants of Doric stock soon began to participate in the colonisation of Sicily. They originated in an area near the isthmus of Corinth, and included people from Megara who founded Megara Hyblaea – possibly as early as the mid-eighth century, to judge from the data brought to light by recent French archaeological excavations – and the Corinthians themselves, who founded Syracuse in 733 BC (according to Thucydides' traditional dating). In the last decades of the eighth century, there was something like a race to lay claim to territory on the peninsula's Ionian coast: 'Achaean' colonies were founded at Sybaris, Croton (Crotone) and Metapontum, as was a Spartan colony at Tarentum (Taranto). Some few decades later, the initial phase of colonisation was completed with the foundation (*ktiseis*) of Gela in Sicily, by settlers from Rhodes and Crete (688); of Locri Epizephyrii, in modern Calabria, by settlers from Locris; and of Siris, between Sybaris and Metapontum, by Asiatic Ionians from Colophon (c. 680–670).

Later in the archaic period, the colonising impulse developed in two directions. On the one hand, numerous secondary settlements developed as the colonists expanded into fresh territories. Examples include Mylae and Himera, sub-colonies of Zancle in

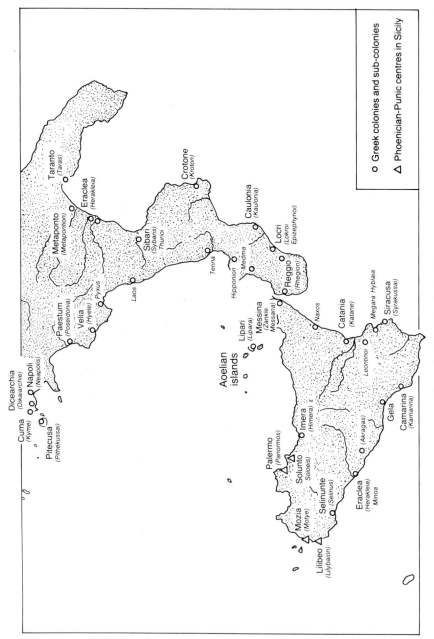

Figure 3 Greek colonisation.

northern Sicily; the southern Sicilian sites of Selinus (Selinunte), settled from Megara Hyblaea (c. 650), Camarina, settled from Syracuse (598) and Agrigentum (Agrigento), settled from Gela (580); Metauros, Medma and Hipponion, on the Tyrrhenian shore of the Calabrian headland, all derived from Locris; Laos, further north on the Tyrrhenian coast, which was a sub-colony of Sybaris; and finally Posidonia, founded by the seventh century by people of Troezenian origin who had come from Sybaris, and thus itself another sub-colony of Sybaris. On the other hand, at some point after the end of the seventh century a fresh wave of colonists set out for the west from the distant and increasingly troubled lands of Asiatic Greece. First to arrive were the Phocaeans, who founded Massalia (Marseilles) on the southern French coast and Alalia in Corsica, before moving down from Alalia to Velia-Elea south of Posidonia (c. 535). They were followed towards the beginning of the sixth century by immigrants from Cnidos and Rhodes who settled at Lipari, and by Samians who are found in Dicaearchia (Pozzuoli) in the Gulf of Naples (c. 530) and in Zancle-Messina early in the fifth century. These later developments will be discussed more fully below.

Modern scholars have failed to agree on the nature and causes of the Greek colonisation as a whole. It is probable that it sprang, especially at first, from commercial interests, including the search for and acquisition of raw materials (particularly metals) and the exchange of products, and also the desire to compete with the sea-voyages of the Phoenicians, as is suggested by the fact that some of the earliest settlements (like Pithecusae) were remote from Greece itself and strategically placed at crossroads of maritime traffic. Such motives would explain the fact that peaceful relations were established with indigenous peoples and that some degree of fusion took place, as the archaeological evidence shows, with the local populations who lived near Greek colonies (for instance, around Sybaris). It is equally likely, however, that demographic pressures played a large role in stimulating colonisation, encouraging some of the population of the mother country to emigrate to new lands and establish permanent settlements there above all with a view to exploiting their agricultural possibilities: so large was the area of workable land occupied by the Greeks in Italy that the country became known as Magna Graecia. One modern discovery of particular relevance here is the existence in the archaic period of large-scale schemes of land-use planning, with geo-metrically laid out fields, in the area near Metapontum – a city whose coinage bore the distinguishing symbol of an ear of wheat. The answer to the question of how the practice originated of designing towns on an orthogonal plan (with straight roads at right angles delineating rectangular areas of land) may lie in the allocation to each family of colonists of its own patch of farmland, as would seem to be indicated by the oldest ground-plan of Megara Hyblaea. It is clear that the need for cultivable land, and all the developments this entailed, led the colonists to extend the territory they occupied and thus provoked conflict with the indigenous inhabitants, who were either enslaved or had to retreat. In other words, colonisation with demographic motives implies territorial domination.

To assess the historical importance of this great colonising movement, we must bear in mind that it rapidly transformed the occupied lands, bringing them up from a proto-historic level (although even at that stage they had been permeated by Mediterranean and eastern influences) to a level of civilisation equal to that attained by the centres of the Greek world. Thenceforth the colonies developed in tandem with the mother cities, reaching the full heights of archaic civilisation, with organised city-states, religious cults brought over from the motherland, stable modes of government, and temples of ever increasing grandeur. Works of art and even (as in the case of Stesichorus of Himera) poems were created. And this is without considering the subsequent development of the Greek world in Italy and Sicily, during the classical and Hellenistic periods.

Alongside their direct effect as centres of civilisation, the colonies also had an indirect effect on the other territories of the Italian region. What counted here was not so much geographical proximity as the responsiveness of the districts and peoples to whom the colonists made approach. Indeed, contact remained partial and superficial in some parts of the hinterland of the colonised area (both in southern Italy and in Sicily), whereas it profoundly and fruitfully affected what we might call the Tyrrhenian area of Italy – Campania, Latium and above all Etruria – which had built up a considerable cultural inheritance of its own. Greek influence, however, did not stem solely from the colonies, but also derived directly from the mother country, short-circuiting the colony.

Corinth, for example, stimulated and affected the centres of Tyrrhenian civilisation more broadly and deeply than can be explained by the influence of a single colonial foundation, even such an important one as Syracuse. This is confirmed by the tradition recorded by the elder Pliny which tells of the establishment of Corinthian artists in Etruria during the seventh century (*Natural History*, XXXV, 36, 152). A large proportion of the proper names taken into Etruscan from Greek mythology seem to be of Corinthian origin; and from Corinth, too, came the mass of imported pottery that was then copied on a large scale locally, as well as figurative motifs and ideas in painting and sculpture and probably also the practice of using terracotta as an architectural material. This practice struck particularly deep roots in Italy, where its use and development continued after the end of the archaic period. Painted vases and artistic ideas and techniques were also imported from Rhodes, from Sparta and especially from Athens, for the Athenians, although they had no part in the colonising movement and no colonial interests, were nonetheless able to establish their commercial supremacy in the Italian pottery market by the first half of the sixth century.

We must mention that the founding of the Greek colonies was paralleled (and perhaps to a certain extent preceded) in the west by that of Phoenician colonies. However, this cannot be said to have rivalled the Greek colonisation in importance or in its effects within the territory of Italy. Indeed, it involved only Italy's westernmost fringes, in the west of Sicily and in Sardinia. In Sicily, the Phoenicians founded the cities of Motya, Palermo and Solunto; in Sardinia, Nora, Bithia, Sulcis, Tharros and Karalis (modern Cagliari). The original commercial motives that led to these first settlements, and the settlements' function as trading-posts, remained unchanged for a long period, and their influence was virtually confined to the indigenous peoples in the immediate vicinity. These cities flourished later, during the period of Carthaginian hegemony; but this marked the start of a new historical epoch, with which we shall deal later.

Etruscan expansion and the remainder of Italy

We have already drawn attention to the possibility that the spread of Villanovan civilisation may indicate an early phase of Etruscan expansion. At the heart of this was of course Etruria itself. Together with the Greek colonisation, it was the most important phenomenon in Italy's history in archaic times, thanks to the speed and extent of its development, the area it affected, and its homogeneous character. In Etruria itself, between the ninth and the seventh centuries aggregations of Villanovan villages expanded into cities among the largest and most splendid not just of Italy but of the entire western central Mediterranean world – cities (to list them from north to south) such as Veii, Caere (Cervèteri), Tarquinii, Vulci, Roselle, Vetulonia, Populonia and Volterra or in the interior, and sometimes at a later date, Volsinii (on whose site Orvieto now stands), Clusium (Chiusi), Perugia, Cortona, Arezzo and Fiesole. Nor is the portrait of Etruria in archaic times complete if we mention only these important cities, for there were in addition many smaller centres and isolated settlements where the presence of monumental sepulchres indicates that an oligarchic and landowning aristocracy came into being.

The fundamental cause of Etruria's economic prosperity, and of the cultural progress that this allowed, lay, as we have already mentioned, in the mineral wealth found there. This was concentrated particularly in the northern coastal region, in the territories of Populonia and Vetulonia, with Elba and the Colline Metallifere ('metal-bearing hills') yielding iron, copper, and ores of silver and lead, but there were other deposits too, such as the iron-mines of the Monti della Tolfa. Metals were in international demand. This must have attracted to Etruria a concentration of entrepreneurs, technicians and workers, including many from overseas. It must have given rise to a complex network of exchange, allowing a vast and ever-growing volume of foreign products to find their way to Etruria. It must, finally, have awakened the political and strategic interest of navigators and colonists, especially the Greeks. It became necessary to deter their ambitions by a strategy of military preparedness at sea – not the least important reason why the Etruscans became a maritime power (or 'thalassocracy'). The great purchasing power of the Etruscan economy, and the rich and powerful citizens' desire for ostentation, encouraged imports from Greece and the Near East. Between the late eighth and early sixth centuries, Villanovan culture entered an extraordinary 'orientalising' period. Many precious materials, such as gold and ivory,

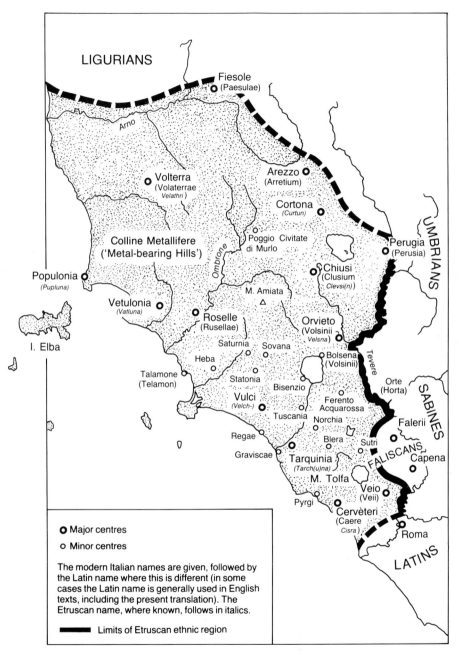

Figure 4 Tyrrhenian Etruria.

were brought in from overseas, as were individual works of craftsmanship – Asian bronzes, Egyptian faience ware, ornamented silver or gilt paterae (libation-dishes) from Syria and Cyprus, magnificent Greek pottery. Also, and above all, sophisticated local artists – metal-workers, goldsmiths, gem-engravers, and so forth – produced articles inspired by the taste for eastern fashions, and here too there must have been large-scale importation of foreign ware made of perishable materials such as wood and, especially, fabrics, which have unfortunately perished. The Greek colonies of Sicily and Magna Graecia show little to match this: it is clear that during the period in question, at any rate, the economic and political circumstances of the Etruscan metropolises were very different from those in the Greek colonies. In Greece itself, moreover, discoveries comparable to those dating from Etruria's orientalising period have been made only in richly endowed shrines, whereas in Etruria they appear to have accumulated essentially in the tombs of socially prominent individuals.

The phenomenon of the orientalising period indicates that the Etruscan coastal waters, and the seas around Italy in general, must have been crowded with merchants, not only from Greece and probably from Phoenicia but also from Etruria itself. Unless appearances of cultural similarity are misleading, there must have been maritime trade between the coasts of Etruria and of the Salerno region from the Villanovan period onwards. There is no reason to be surprised that the Etruscans had made their naval presence felt so far to the south when we recall that the historian Ephorus (Strabo VI, 2, 2) refers to Tyrrhenian pirates as being active along the eastern Sicilian coastline before the establishment of the Greek colonies. Etruscan piracy is a common motif of Greek literature, from the 'Homeric' hymn to Dionysus. However, the privateering of those days must obviously have been largely guerilla warfare at sea, with offensive forays and battles of attrition between rival powers and forces. Within the Greek colonial world itself, Zancle was reputedly founded by 'pirates' from Cumae, probably in an attempt to block the passage of Etruscan 'pirates' through the Straits of Messina.

For all coastal trade along the Tyrrhenian seaboard and for any maritime operations directed towards Sicily, the ports of call of Campania must have been of the first importance. With its easy

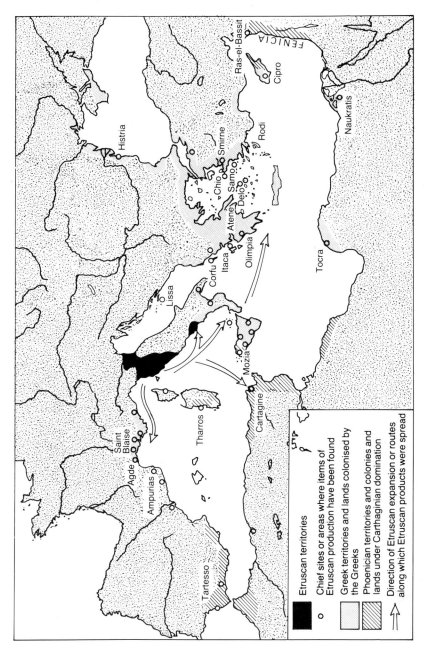

Figure 5 Etruscan commercial expansion in the Mediterranean (seventh century and first half of sixth century BC).

landings and fertile soil, this region seems to have acquired its pivotal role between the zones of Etruscan and Greek expansion at the very beginning of the historical era. The Etruscans established contacts along the littoral of the Gulf of Salerno, where Ponte-cagnano was the most important centre (or at any rate the one of which we have the best knowledge) and where the 'colony' of Marcina was sited: its whereabouts remain uncertain, but it may have been at Vietri. They then consolidated their rule and extended it to the peninsula of Sorrento and to the Sarno delta, at Castellamare and Pompeii. Thence they penetrated the entire plain of Campania, until they abutted on the Greek colonies of the Gulf of Naples, where their cities flourished well into the historical era: Nocera, Nola, Acerra, Suessula and especially Capua, which became the capital of Etruscan Campania.

All this is enough to suggest that the maritime activity of the Etruscans must have been widespread and formidable. We can assume that its scale increased as the Villanovan period gave way to the orientalising phase. Sources in classical literature refer explicitly to Etruscan dominion over the seas or thalassocracy, mentioning their presence not only in Campania, in the Lipari or Aeolian islands, on the Sicilian coast, in Sardinia and Corsica, but even in the Balearic Islands and Spain. However, these fragment-ary references, vague and sometimes suspect, do not readily allow us to establish either the chronology or the actual geographical scope of events. Discoveries of Etruscan artefacts (in particular, bucchero ware, painted vases in the Etrusco-Corinthian style and amphorae) have been made along the coasts of the Italian peninsula, in the large islands enclosing the Tyrrhenian sea, in the coastal centres of southern France and Spain, at Carthage, and also in Greece and other eastern Mediterranean areas. In themselves, these prove only the wide extent of trading contacts, in which Etruria, predominantly an importer of manufactured goods, was also to a limited extent an exporter; and indirect transfer may, and in many cases must, have been involved. However, there is some coincidence between the whereabouts of these import markets, especially in the west, and the references in the literary sources, and this suggests that the Etruscans may have made voyages beyond the sphere of the Tyrrhenian sea, even if they did not establish their dominion outside it. Most of these exported items date from between the end of the seventh and the early decades of the sixth century, and would thus appear to have at least partially predated the founding of Massalia (Marseilles) by the Phocaeans (c. 600 BC). All the evidence indicates that the Etruscan thalassocracy enjoyed its most active and expansive phase no later than the seventh century, at a time when the Greeks were still developing and consolidating the methods by which they were to establish a colonial presence in the west, and when Phoenician colonisation had not yet acquired the energetic single-mindedness that it gained under the impulse of Carthaginian hegemony.

Alongside this maritime expansion, the Etruscans extended their influence on the Italian mainland. We must obviously not be carried away by some of the claims made by classical writers, such as Cato's famous remark (in Servius, *ad Aen.*, XI, 584) that 'in Tuscorum iure pene omnis Italia fuerat' ('almost the whole of Italy had been under the dominion of the Etruscans') – a remark echoed, more cautiously but with more circumstantial detail, by Livy (I, 2; V, 33), who records that by land and sea, from the Alps to the Straits of Messina, the Etruscans were renowned, powerful, and wealthy. Nor should we envisage an Etruscan empire, a kind of early attempt to unify the peninsula in anticipation of the later Roman conquest. The first stages of expansion, lost as they are in the twilight of proto-history, should probably be thought of as a series of individual moves largely inspired by the wish to secure economic and commercial control – though such moves must have been fraught with political and military implications, and would have entailed a certain cultural prestige. Some increase in activity by land must also have resulted from the expansion of Etruscan maritime interests. At all events, it is certain (from the eloquent testimony of classical historiography and from data acquired in the fields of archaeology, the study of inscriptions and place-names, and so forth) that the Etruscans occupied and held sway over lands beyond the confines of their home territory between the course of the Tiber and the Tuscan-Emilian ridge of the Apennines. These lands included Latium and Campania (or at any rate substantial parts of these regions) and, beyond the Apennines, Emilia and Romagna; there was also some penetration, fairly short-lived and difficult to specify with any certainty, beyond the Po and along the Ligurian coast.

Contrary to what we might logically expect, the Etruscans established a presence in neighbouring Latium (by which is meant the Latium of the ancients, lying to the south of the Tiber) only after they had done so in more distant Campania. This is explained by the overriding importance of their maritime interests, which as we have noted led them from very early on to make landfalls on the coasts of lower Campania. Only later, and probably partly in order to consolidate and extend their dominions in Campania, did they feel it necessary to secure a further unbroken line of communication across Latium (which lay between Etruria and Campania) by the inland route via the Sacco and Liris river-valleys. While not obliging them to conquer the entire territory, this did imply control of the chief towns and thoroughfares. Signs of this are to be found in the orientalising grave-goods of the princely tombs at Palestrina (the Praeneste of antiquity), which seem to indicate the presence of Etruscan dynasts. The finds date from the first half of the seventh century; there is also an inscription in Etruscan. Other related finds of more or less the same date have been made at Lavinium and Satricum. As for Rome, tradition holds that an Etruscan monarchy was established there in 616 BC, when Lucius Tarquinius Priscus, a native of Tarquinii, came to power. Without casting doubt on this date (which is only an approximation), we should note that it is rather late in relation to the other indications of the Etruscan presence in Latium that we have just mentioned. This lateness is all the more surprising given that Rome was nearer to Etruria than the other places. However, it may be explained by the fact that since the eighth century Rome had been an outpost of Sabine penetration. The Sabines, of eastern Italic stock, had made their way down the Tiber valley, and may well have posed a major obstacle to Etruscan advance (we should recall here that Tarquinius Priscus' predecessor was traditionally held to have been Ancus Marcius, a king of Sabine race, and that many of Tarquinius Priscus' military operations were directed against the Sabines). The period which, still following tradition, we can call the reign of Tarquinius Priscus, between the end of the seventh century and the first decades of the sixth, saw the 'making' of Rome in archaeological terms. The first monumental buildings were erected, for instance the Regia and Comitia in the Forum, and according to literary sources the temple of Jove in the Capitol and the city walls were built. The use of terracotta building materials and the presence of objects typical of the late orientalising phase clearly reveal Etruscan influence. There is no reason to doubt the historical existence of the king, his wife

Tanaquil (the name is typically Etruscan), or the founders of the Tarquinian dynasty in general. It is probable that an aristocracy of Etruscan origin established itself at the foot of the Campidoglio in the area later called the *vicus Tuscus*, not far from where (within the precincts of S. Omobono) a small ivory plaque has been discovered, fashioned like a lion and inscribed with the name of Araz Silqetenas Spurianas, who may himself have come from Tarquinii. But Etruscan inscriptions are lacking, while on the *Lapis Niger* (a cippus or small column in the Roman Forum), a public monument bearing sacred prescriptions for the ruler of the Comitia dateable to this same period, Latin is the language used, indicating that Etruscan influence was only partial.

More complex problems arise when we turn to the dominions of the Etruscans in northern Italy. Classical writers envisaged these as a full-scale colonisation in form and method, with twelve cities matching the *dodekápolis* of Tyrrhenian Etruria. This colonisation was thought to have taken place in the distant past, as can be seen from the legend of Tarchon, the heroic founder of Tarquinii. We have already expressed the view that around Bologna and in Romagna (at Verucchio, San Marino) we should recognise Etruscan elements dating back to the beginning of the Iron Age. These are evident in the local Villanovan culture, which is clearly an intrusion deriving from the Tyrrhenian region. The widespread theory of an Etruscan 'conquest' no earlier than the later sixth century now seems contradicted by evidence including the identification of an Etruscan inscription on a late Villanovan vase from Bologna dateable to approximately 600 BC. It is interesting that Livy records a tradition that, at around this time, the Etruscans were defeated by Gauls who broke into the Po plain very near the Ticino river: this suggests that the Etruscans entertained expansive designs at that early date and in those distant parts. They may indeed have done so. The advent of the 'Certosa' phase of Etruscan civilisation, succeeding the late Villanovan Arnoaldi phase, can be attributed to an upsurge of Etruscan activity beyond the Apennines. This was related to the new and major importance the Etruscans now attached to the Adriatic estuaries, because of the economic and political crisis in the Tyrrhenian region (about which we shall have more to say later). It involved intense colonising activity and led to the founding of such cities as Felsina (modern Bologna), Marzabotto and Spina. This, too, we shall discuss later.

At this point, it may be of interest to review the situation in the rest of Italy, peninsular and continental, and the condition of its inhabitants. We reveal a certain historical prejudice in the way we conceive the problem of relations between colonists and indigenous populations. This applies particularly in the case of the Greeks who settled on the coasts of southern Italy, but it also applies, and in largely similar terms, to the Etruscans, especially where the latter appeared as sea-borne colonists (as they did in Campania and perhaps in Liguria). Inland encounters between the Etruscans and non-Etruscan peoples constitute a more complex theme. These took place along the boundaries marked out by rivers, such as the Tiber – which from the beginning generally encouraged the separation (apart from the Faliscan enclave) of the Etruscans from the Latins, Sabines and Umbrians – or the Po and Adige, which divided them from the Veneti. The Venetic city of Este, set among the Euganean hills, stood on the far side of the plain opposite Villanovan-Etruscan Bologna on the slopes of the Apennines. The basic picture is of a dialectical interaction, fraught with historical implications and consequences, between the coastal immigrants with their organising and civilising energies and the inland dwellers whose way of life had remained arrested at a late prehistoric level. This dialectic took the form of a range of cultural influences exerted by the newcomers, which the local peoples in time imitated, readily or sluggishly; of more or less extensive and significant movement by the settlers into the hinterland, by way of the river-valleys (a pattern typical of Basilicata and Campania); and of the fascination which the fabled civilisation of the coast came to hold for the simple inhabitants of the mountains. All this was to give rise to the large-scale movements of reaction typical of the second phase of Italy's pre-Roman history.

The inhabitants of the Adriatic coast now begin to appear in the light of history, developing the beginnings of a distinctive ethnic consciousness and showing some cultural individuality. To the south, in Apulia, the Iapygians or Apuli, who had inherited an advanced palaeo-Italic culture and whose geographical position had exposed them from early times to influences from the Mediterranean and trans-Adriatic world, now drew on this experience to attain a fairly advanced level of proto-urban (and, later, fully urban) organisation, of geometric decoration and of figurative art (such as we see in the astonishing array of funerary stelae recently brought to light in the area around Sipontum in Foggia province). At the same time, however, they preserved a certain isolation, in the archaic period and later, vis-à-vis what must have been the powerfully pervasive influence of the nearby centres of Greek colonisation, particularly Tarentum – and this detachment, as we shall see, also took the form of political hostility. The central region was inhabited by the authors of what has traditionally been called the 'Picenian' culture, now more appropriately known as the Middle Adriatic. This flourished between the eighth and the fifth centuries. It was very receptive to orientalising and archaic Greek influences, which may in some cases have reached it via the Etruscans. Among its characteristic features during relatively late times was a clumsy type of sculpture in stone, of which the most typical instance is the famous warrior of Capestrano. This population is now thought to have consisted chiefly of the most advanced members of the eastern Italic peoples, and more specifically the Sabines, a view supported especially by epigraphic and linguistic evidence. To the north, the Veneti seem to have lived in their own self-contained world, loyal to their ethnic, cultural and territorial traditions, from the beginning of the Iron Age until the Roman conquest. Among the artefacts they have left us are examples of the special style of figurative embossed bronze work, found also among other Alpine peoples, typical of the 'situla culture'; these reveal central European, orientalising Etruscan and Greek influences. The peoples of the peninsular hinterland, whether of Oenotrian-Ausonian, Iapygian or eastern Italic stock, were subject to a variety of influences, from the Greek Mezzogiorno and from the Tyrrhenian and Adriatic worlds. Their own culture had not, as yet, acquired any definite shape. Where they had come into contact with sophisticated aesthetic models, they sometimes reproduced them in cruder and more primitive versions, sometimes took them over intact, and sometimes developed them in an eclectic manner such as is seen in the remarkable flowering during the archaic period of Melfi in the western territory of the Daunians (present-day Basilicata). But this world as a whole was still, historically speaking, passive. The hour of its awakening was soon to strike.

East Greek influences and the development of the Greek colonies and Tyrrhenian cities

The final wave of voyages and colonial expeditions from Greece began at the end of the seventh century, bringing the Samians and Phocaeans of eastern Greece to the west and opening a new phase in the story of archaic Italy. With the founding of Massalia and the other trading centres of the Gulf of Lyons a virtual second front was created immediately adjacent to the Etruscan navy's home waters, and this reduced Etruscan pressure on the southern Tyrrhenian region. Meanwhile, the Carthaginians were beginning to take over the whole varied legacy of the Phoenicians' colonial ventures in the west. The most westerly part of the Mediterranean, and its access routes, was brought entirely under Carthaginian control. The end of the Etruscan thalassocracy's period of expansion, which also marked the start of its decline, is symbolised by two events. There is, first of all, the story recounted by Diodorus Siculus (V, 19ff) of how the Carthaginians barred the way to an Etruscan colonial expedition in search of a fabulously fertile island lying in the Atlantic beyond the Pillars of Hercules. This episode was not dated, and may be of a somewhat legendary character. There is also the establishment, around 500 BC, of a colony settled from Rhodes and Cnidos on the Aeolian islands, which became a kind of Greek rampart protecting Sicily and the Straits. The strategic importance of those settlements is attested by the fact that the Etruscans struggled long and hard to seize control of the archipelago from the Lipari-based colonists. They launched numerous attacks (according to the account in Strabo, VI, 2, 10), probably throughout the sixth century and after, but these were repeatedly repulsed. The historical sources fully reflect this struggle, and we even have epigraphic testimony of it in the inscribed votive gifts left by inhabitants of Lipari at the shrine at Delphi.

These first, dynamic exploratory and colonial expeditions, carried out by Greeks, Phoenicians and Etruscans and culminating in the far-reaching ventures of the Asiatic Greeks from the distant frontiers of the Hellenic world, now gradually ceased. A phase of consolidation followed. Commercial and political spheres of influence were marked out, by sea and land. In other words, a balance seems to have been struck, within the Italic area in the broad sense and especially in the Tyrrhenian region, between the powers of the Greek and Etruscan cities and those of the Carthaginians. This equilibrium was complex and unstable, as we shall see below, but it was sufficient to promote a tradition of ever-growing diplomatic, religious, cultural, artistic and economic relationships, to create a truly international way of life, to spread common civilising influences, and to allow the various centres, irrespective of ethnic affiliation, to reach very high levels of development.

It is a fact of some interest, and of definite historical importance, that the progress made by these communities in Italy during the sixth century and the form taken by many of the common features of their civilisation were shaped by an increase in direct contacts with the eastern Greek world, especially Ionia. Pioneers, traders and colonists began to arrive in more or less numerous and organised expeditions, in the wake of the sailors who first embarked in well-equipped long-distance vessels from Phocaea, in Aeolia, along the route opened up by the illustrious voyage of the 'Samian' ship of Kolaios, to 'discover' the Adriatic region, Etruria, Iberia and Tartessus (Herodotus, I, 163). Apart from this, regular commercial shipping routes were established and friendly relations developed, for instance the very close bonds linking Sybaris and Miletus. Culturally important figures moved about and migrated within this world, as we see in the examples of the poet Ibycus, from Reggio, entertained for some time in Samos by the tyrant Polycrates, or (the most famous case) of Pythagoras, who made the reverse journey (around 530 BC), leaving Samos to settle permanently in Italy. Ionian artists and craftsmen were certainly to be found in the flourishing cities of the west, above all in Etruria, and in some cases evidence of their handiwork has survived, in the shape of *hydriae* or water-jars made at Caere. Finally, merchandise was traded, and in particular East Greek works of art and craft were imported in large quantities, especially vases (notably the cups with painted bands found all over Italy) and fabrics (which have perished, but to which there are many references in the sources), as well as other valuable figurative works which helped to introduce new tastes and fashions.

The art of Ionia was soft, inventive, inclined to realism. During the second half of the century, as it replaced the more angular and schematic modes of the Daedalic-Peloponnesian tradition in painting and sculpture almost everywhere, it tended to endow the figurative language of Magna Graecia and Italy with common traits. The new style found a particularly favourable, or congenial, reception in Etruria. Sophistication, luxury, a certain effeminacy and Asiatic *habrosyne* – these grew fashionable among the upper classes of the Etruscan cities, becoming proverbially associated with Sybaris and Siris, and we see them reflected in the costumes worn by the figures in the pictures discovered at Tarquinii. It seems fair to assume that the religious and intellectual life of the most thriving communities on the Tyrrhenian and Ionian seaboards was likewise infused with influences from East Greek civilisation, which would have been to some degree permeated by the spirit of the great archaic Ionian tradition, with its poetry, scientific curiosity and speculative temper. Indeed, Pythagoras' teaching at Croton was itself among the great events in this common Greek-Tyrrhenian cultural *koiné*, which had germinated under the shared influence of Ionia. Pythagoras achieved great renown, and his followers constituted a remarkable school, whose doctrine exerted great influence, both socially and politically. Students came not only from Magna Graecia and Sicily but also from as far afield as Etruria and Rome. Even King Numa Pompilius was enrolled, according to some admittedly anachronistic traditional accounts, among the disciples of the Samian philosopher. This marked the beginnings of what Aristotle called the 'Italic school'. Almost at the same time, with the re-founding of Velia (see below), another strand of Ionian thought reached Italy, as Xenophanes of Colophon prepared the ground for the impressive philosophical flowering of the Eleatic school.

All this activity was based upon the economic prosperity attained by the southern Italian colonies and the cities of the Tyrrhenian littoral. The historical record is obviously far less detailed than for the Greek world of the same era and, for the non-Hellenic centres (with the sole exception of Rome), we have no more than broad general indications. Yet, speaking in general terms, the better documentation afforded by historical sources and inscriptions enables us to discern the main characteristics of the history of the area. We may catch a glimpse of the vicissitudes of these communities, of their mutual rivalries, expansionary ventures or attempts at domination, of their domestic politics, passage of laws, modes of governing the *polis*, social and political developments and conflicts.

On present evidence, certain cities seem to have been especially important in terms of their size, profusion of monuments, or demographic, economic or political significance. On the Ionian coast these were (from east to west) Tarentum, Metapontum, Siris, Sybaris, Croton and Locri; in the Straits, Reggio; and on the Tyrrhenian coast, Posidonia (Paestum), Caere, Tarquinii, Vulci and Populonia. These cities generally succeeded in protecting and extending their trade by sea, continually finding new markets for their agricultural produce and manufactures, and establishing a territorial hinterland which they ruled or protected. Since the colonies of Magna Graecia, even when their inhabitants were of the same racial stock (as with the Achaeans), do not appear to have established any stable system of cooperation, they naturally tended to be drawn into struggles for supremacy. South of the isthmus, in present-day Calabria (the original and authentic 'Italy'), Reggio and Locri dominated, especially following the defeat on the river Sagra of the inhabitants of Croton at the hands of the Locrians assisted by the people of Reggio (around the middle of the sixth century). At about the same time, the cities of the gulf defeated and destroyed the Ionian centre of Siris. This allowed Sybaris, in particular, to establish and consolidate its leading position among the Achaean colonies, to impose its supremacy over an extensive territory that reached the shores of the Tyrrhenian Sea (where Laos, Pyxous and Posidonia were reliable allies), and to bring its influence to bear as far afield as the Campanian border. It thus became the major power in the peninsular Mezzogiorno.

The zenith of Sybaris' fortunes in Magna Graecia accompanied, and probably also favoured, the pre-eminence of Caere and Vulci in Etruria. The history of archaic Italy in the earlier and middle part of the sixth century is characterised by the rise to power of these cities, which attained in some ways a pan-Mediterranean importance. The archaeological evidence, as well as what we can infer from traditional accounts, suggests that Tarquinii and Vetulonia had flourished economically earlier, during the eighth and seventh centuries. They may have enjoyed a corresponding political and economic importance. But the prestige of Caere then increased until it outshone and eclipsed its rivals. This is borne out by the wealth of monumental remains at Caere dating from the middle and late phase of the orientalising period, which are paralleled by similar finds in the hinterland and in Latium. Evidence of the vigour of Vulci during the first half of the sixth century is found in the large scale on which its pottery was exported, not just within Etruria but to Rome and Carthage. The power-struggle in southern Etruria and Latium is reflected in the literary, epigraphic and figurative sources (above all the paintings in the François tomb at Vulci) which tell of the campaign of the brothers Aulus and Caelius Vibenna (Aule and Caile Vipinas) and their comrade Mastarna (Macstrna) against the Tarquinii of Rome and the chieftains allied with them, a campaign which led to their taking power for a time at Rome. The Emperor Claudius recorded a tradition identifying Mastarna with the king Servius Tullius.

Struggles for control of the Tyrrhenian Sea

In the wider international arena, the balance of power that appears to have been struck between the cities of southern Etruria and Magna Graecia was to be undermined from without by the Phocaeans and the Carthaginians. The former had founded the colony of Alalia on the eastern coast of Corsica, and their numbers had been reinforced by people who fled Phocaea when it was taken by the Persians (545 BC). They now posed an immediate threat to the seas and coastlands opposite Etruria. They may well also have found themselves in conflict with the Carthaginians for control of Sardinia, which from early times (at least since the eighth century) had been partly colonised by Phoenicians: the place-name of Olbia, on Sardinia's north-east coast, would confirm this possibility if it does indeed reflect a Phocaean attempt at settlement. The outcome was a military coalition between the Etruscans (comprising, or led by, Caere) and the Carthaginians. Each contributed sixty ships to the naval force which did battle with the Phocaean fleet, also of sixty ships, in the Sea of Sardinia (possibly in the region of the Bocche di Bonifacio between Sardinia and Corsica). This memorable battle is described by Herodotus (I, 166), who says that for the Greeks it was a 'Cadmian victory'. In its aftermath, Alalia was in fact abandoned, probably on the grounds that it was impossible to defend. The Phocaeans left it and travelled by sea to the Reggio area, where they tried in vain to settle, moving on to the coastal region of the Cilento. Here, presumably with the consent of their near neighbours at Posidonia, they founded the colony of Velia.

In this way, a division of spheres of influence was arrived at (though some doubts have recently been raised about this). The Etruscans occupied at least the eastern coast of Corsica, establishing a colony with the Greek name Nicaea, perhaps on the site of Alalia itself. The Carthaginians had a free hand in Sardinia. However, Sardinia proved extremely difficult to conquer, for the indigenous inhabitants, the Ilienses, put up a determined resistance. Archaeological evidence indicates that the Ilienses were a quite highly developed people: their fortresses, towns and shrines all boasted monumental architecture during the early centuries of the first millennium BC, the most flourishing period of this Sardinian civilisation, with its *nuraghi* or stone towers. A Carthaginian expedition under Malchos (? 'the king'), which set out around the middle of the sixth century, was unsuccessful, and only towards the end of the century was the subjugation of the island completed, a troublesome task in which leading roles were played by Mago's sons, Hasdrubal and Hamilcar. Some indigenous communities or federations of communities may at this time have made diplomatic overtures aimed at securing the aid of the Italian Greeks, as can be inferred from the inscription on a bronze plaque found at Olympia, which mentions the *entente* reached between Sybaris and its allies and the 'Serdaioi', under the patronage of the city of Posidonia (although the reference here may be not to the Sardinians but to some other similarly-named people or city). If there was some bond between the Sardinians and Sybaris, it is possible that the fall of the latter city in 510 BC may have made it easier for Mago's sons to complete the conquest of the island, for the dates match. There are also some further indications of the interest the Greeks took in Sardinia and of the relations they established with its inhabitants. When the Persians conquered Asia Minor and the Phocaeans were fleeing to Corsica, Biantis put forward a scheme for the colonisation of the island by a pan-Ionian expedition. This came to nothing. Fifty years later, however, during the Ionian revolt, Histaeus recalled the project, an old dream now ruled out by the Carthaginian occupation of Sardinia. Legend persistently connected the Sardinian world with such heroes of Greek mythology as Aristaeus and Daedalus.

In this same period, Carthage imposed its *epikráteia* or territorial dominion not only on Sardinia but on western Sicily. Here, the indigenous inhabitants, the Elymi, would seem to have concurred in what was plainly an anti-Greek move. This laid the foundations for the conflict between Carthaginians and Greeks in Sicily – a conflict which lasted almost three hundred years and had profound consequences for the history of Italy in antiquity. The establishment of stable spheres of control, by land and sea, involved a series of struggles for strategic points and a series of alliances, stable for a time but then shifting as the conflict entered a new phase.

It is in the context of this bloc politics that we must understand the historical accounts (especially the famous passage in Aristotle, *Politics*, III, 9, 1280a) of the treaties between the Etruscans and the Carthaginians. The existence of such ties is confirmed by the abundance of Etruscan artefacts at Carthage. These include an inscription in which the latter city is named (and further verification is provided by the gold plaque with an inscription in Phoenician found at Pyrgi, discussed below). Generally friendly relations, joint ventures and specific pacts were probably all involved, throughout a long period from the sixth to the fourth century. The basis was a common interest in opposing the military and commercial might of the Greeks. But for that very reason, we should not assume that any firm and stable understanding was established. As early as the archaic period the cities of Etruria may sometimes have acted together in political association, and this may even have been formally embodied in some sort of *koinon* analogous to that among the city-states of Asiatic Ionia, from whom the Etruscan civilisation borrowed so much (we know that such a formal alliance existed later, when the Etruscan states held their 'congress' at the Fanum Voltumnae). For all that, they were independent *poleis*, and sometimes fell out among themselves. Separate diplomatic relations must have existed, at any rate in form, between each Etruscan city and Carthage – itself a single *polis* even if it was also already the capital of a large empire. Domestic factions, pursuing ends of their own, may have complicated the situation. We can reasonably assume that the great rivalry between Greeks and Carthaginians evoked varying responses. Alongside the natural convergence of interests which we see in the war against the Phocaeans of Alalia, countervailing particular interests must have come into play – for instance where valuable commercial contacts were involved, or where people were swayed by feelings of loyalty or respect towards the Greek world with its cultural and religious prestige. Hesitations of this kind were expressed, perhaps, when the inhabitants of Caere carried out solemn rites of expiation, as commanded by the Delphic oracle, following the massacre of Phocaean prisoners after the calamitous battle of the Sardinian Sea (the account, again, is in Herodotus). It is noteworthy that Etruscan *thesaurói* and gifts are found at Delphi and Olympia.

The growing power of Carthage may at times have allowed the Carthaginians to impose their own political priorities, if not their outright supremacy, not just on the island inhabitants but on peninsular communities too. Carthaginian ships may have raided or threatened the Italian coast. The understanding between the Etruscan and Punic worlds cannot always have been an accord between equals, for the Etruscans found their freedom of strategic and naval action increasingly curbed. After the battle of the Sardinian Sea, and as a result of their repeated reverses in the Aeolian islands, they were restricted to their home waters in the northern Tyrrhenian. Evidence of this is found in the provisions of the one treaty between a Tyrrhenian city (linked to the Etruscan sphere) and Carthage whose text – from a document in an archaic script and language – is preserved in historical tradition. This is the first treaty between Carthage and Rome (Polybius, III, 22), which can now be dated with some certainty to the last quarter of the sixth century. It implies that there was a degree of free trade and passage in the Tyrrhenian, while there were restrictions in the seas bordering Sardinia and Africa, and the western Mediterranean was completely out of bounds. It also refers to Carthaginian raids on the coast of Latium. Direct Carthaginian political influence over Etruria, if not the existence of a Carthaginian protectorate, is probably to be discerned in the dedication by the 'king' of Caere, Thefarie Velianas, of a 'sacred place' in the sanctuary of Pyrgi to the Phoenician goddess Astarte. This is recorded in the bilingual Phoenician-Etruscan text of the gold plaques discovered at Pyrgi.

The Etruscans, either on their own account or within the framework of military cooperation with Carthage, continued to entertain designs in the southern Tyrrhenian throughout the last decades of the sixth and the beginning of the fifth centuries. The Etruscan attack in force on Cumae (525 BC, according to the 'Cumaean chronicle' of Dionysus of Halicarnassus, VII,3) was an attempt to cut the noose gradually tightening around Etruria. It

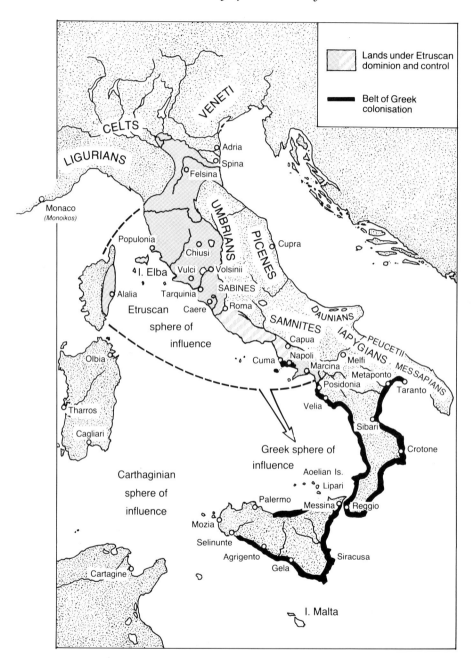

Figure 6 **Spheres of influence towards the end of the sixth century BC.**

was aimed at Campania, the strategic nerve-centre of the whole Tyrrhenian region. It is worth mentioning that the expedition is said to have involved northern Etruscans, Umbrians and even Daunians from Apulia, probably as mercenaries. Had it succeeded, the most northerly of the major Greek colonies on the Tyrrhenian coast would have been eliminated, and with it the barrier which had for so long prevented the Etruscans from expanding southwards. The Etruscans might then have been able to pursue a new strategy in the peninsula, involving the peoples of the hinterland in an encirclement of the Greek colonial centres – principally Sybaris and its allies. The failure of the expedition may thus be explained in part by support given to Cumae by neighbouring cities. Distant naval actions directed at Sicily (apart from the Lipari islands) are associated, rather hazily, with the campaigns of Dorieus the Spartan in western Sicily (c. 510 BC). Returning to Campania, one can imagine other attacks being launched against Cumae by the Etruscan cities between the late sixth and early fifth centuries, attacks which culminated in failure with the final naval battle of 474 BC.

Institutional developments and political disruption: the period of the tyrants

The end of the sixth century and the close of the archaic period were marked by crisis throughout the Italian region. This was rooted not only in the developing international situation reviewed above, but also in the processes forming and transforming the social and institutional character of the cities of the Greek-Tyrrhenian world which had played a key role in the history of archaic Italy.

It is hard to obtain a clear picture of the social and political organisation of the colonies at the time of their foundation and in early times generally. The same applies to the non-Hellenic communities of Campania, Latium and Etruria, which were constituting themselves as *poleis* in imitation of the Greek cities (such detailed data as we have here are retrospective and of rather doubtful authenticity, and are found only in sources concerned with the early history of Rome). There is no doubt that socio-political forms differed widely. It can be assumed, however, that the concentration of wealth – especially landed wealth – and power in the hands of certain families (*gene* or *gentes*) gave these city-states a generally aristocratic character: such concentration, common in contemporary Greek civilisation, had probably taken place in Tyrrhenian Italy too by the beginning of the urban period, if not earlier. In the Greek colonies, monarchies of the archaic kind had disappeared or were disappearing, but there are good grounds for believing that they continued to exist for a long while in Etruria and the other indigenous centres. Monarchy had functional attributes (hereditary or elected chieftains had sacred powers and supreme military authority) as well as pomp and splendour (a golden crown, the *toga praetexta*, a throne of ivory, the rods or *fasces*, and other insignia which the Etruscans bequeathed to the magistrates of Rome) that may have been partly influenced by eastern models.

The gradual attainment of a rule of law (brought about everywhere in the Greek world through the work of the legislators between the seventh and sixth centuries), the revolutionary introduction of the hoplites, the claims advanced by the *demos*, political struggle, the rise of the tyrants – all these developments affected the western Greek world, which participated and indeed in some respects led the way in them. Traditional accounts tell, for instance, of the laws made by Zaleucus at Locri and of the activity of Andromadas and Charondas at Reggio. We must assume that these influences, refracted by local conditions, affected the politico-institutional development of Italy's non-Hellenic cities too. The historians of Rome mention Servius Tullius' constitutional reforms, the fall of the Tarquinian monarchy and the institution of the Republic, and the existence of sole supreme magistracies of proto-republican type, different from the college of two consuls (*magister populi, praetor maximus*). All this reflects the far-reaching processes which during the sixth century undoubtedly affected not just Rome but, earlier and more intensely, all the great Etruscan cities which held political and cultural sway in the Tyrrhenian region. The scale and vitality of overseas trade and the development of production must have brought a new mercantile class to the fore. Its power was asserted within the structure of the state in ordinances specifying property qualifications for the ruling class (such as we find in Solon's Athens and in the Roman system of centuries attributed to Servius Tullius). The old institutions of monarchy must have suffered various fates. Unfortunately, we

cannot establish any detailed picture; but they clearly lost importance or were replaced by elective temporary magistracies. The
citizens must have become aware of their rights as a more or less
constituted body (in the sense of the *demos* or *populus*) alongside
councils of elders dominated by the old aristocracy; and these new
powers must have been gained, at times, through violent conflicts
tending to favour regimes of personal power more or less similar to
those of the Greek tyrants.

The movement from primitive oligarchies and monarchies to
constitutional structures favouring a more equal sharing of power,
and to the rule of tyrants, was a historical phenomenon common to
the entire Italian area. It must have varied according to place and
circumstance – now swift and now slow, taking the form of a
revolution here and of a gradual development there, and sometimes involving halts, turnings back and compromise solutions.
For instance, a kind of tempered oligarchy is reflected in the
constitutions of some Greek cities: Charondas is said to have
provided Reggio with such a constitution before Anaxilas established his tyranny. Within the *polis*, mutually opposed tendencies
and parties must have come into being and organised themselves,
sometimes remaining in conflict for long periods. Cities with
different types of regime must also have taken up opposing
ideological positions. The dialectic of internal institutional
developments often affected the conduct of foreign policy and the
struggle for hegemony. It directly influenced the course of events
towards the end of the sixth century, which saw the destruction of
the balance established between Etruria and Magna Graecia during
the previous decades.

The most striking case in point is the downfall of Sybaris. At the
height of its hegemonic power, prosperous, sophisticated, open to
fresh cultural influences, Sybaris had, thanks to its economic
vitality, a fluid social structure allowing rapid mobility. It may also
have been influenced by Miletus, the most advanced and turbulent
polis of Ionia, with which it enjoyed friendly relations and which
offered an example of progressive ferment and intense political
struggle. Sybaris was the scene of much innovation and experi-
ment, which culminated in the well-known tyranny of Telys, with
its pronounced democratic overtones. This inevitably aroused the
antagonism of the oligarchic regimes of the other cities of Magna
Graecia, on the lookout for an opportunity to challenge Sybaris'

supremacy. The leading role fell to Croton, the centre of
Pythagoras' teaching, legislation and organisation. The Pythagorean programme, conservative in temper and favouring austere
behaviour in both public and private spheres, was propagated and
sustained through a mystical and fanatical veneration for the
master's person. Political interests fuelled a surge of moral fervour,
war broke out between Croton and Sybaris, and the latter city was
not just defeated but utterly and pitilessly destroyed (510 BC).

This fateful event caused upheaval in Greece and left a void in
Italy. A whole series of other occurrences accompanied and
succeeded it, transforming Italy's political complexion at the end of
the archaic period. Tyrannical regimes established themselves
almost everywhere, not long after their advent in the mother
country. Sybaris remained a strong influence, despite the city's fall
and even as a reaction to it. Victorious Croton itself was repeatedly
shaken by anti-oligarchic and anti-Pythagorean movements, culminating in a popular uprising in whose course the quarters of the
Pythagorean *hetairia* (brotherhood) were burned to the ground,
Kylon established his demagogic regime, and the philosopher
himself was exiled, to die at Metapontum. Democratic forces
helped install the tyrant Aristodemus (at Cumae in the final years
of the sixth century) and Anaxilas the Messenian (at Reggio, from
494 BC), and during this same period Aristophilides ruled
Tarentum, along more traditional lines, as 'king'. In Greek Sicily,
apart from earlier tyrannical regimes of which little is known for
certain, Cleandrus and Hippocrates established their personal rule
at Gela, which enjoyed dominion over much of the eastern part of
the island during the late sixth and early fifth centuries. Their
successor, Gelon, founded the dynasty of the Deinomenids at
Syracuse (485 BC).

Similar developments must have taken place as the non-Hellenic
cities imitated their Greek neighbours. We now turn again to the
area of Etruria, Latium and Campania, which – even apart from the
fact that we are dealing with the period and the problems involved
in the earliest history of Rome – was now assuming a role of greater
importance in the development of the whole Italian world.
Archaeological and historical sources support the view, held by
most modern historians, that during the last decades of the sixth
century, Rome, under Etruscan dominion and influence, reached
as high a level of development as the major centres of the southern

coast of Etruria. It is probable that the foreign and domestic turmoil of the 'Servian' period was followed by a temporary consolidation or re-establishment of the old Tarquinian monarchy: classical tradition reflects this in its references to the reign of Tarquinius Superbus (534–509 BC). There may also be some historical warrant for the notion that Rome exercised its supremacy over Latium in that the princes and chieftains of various Latin settlements (Octavius Mamilius at Tusculum, Tullius Herdonius at Aricia, Sextus Tarquinius at Gabii, and so on) were dependants of the king of Rome. At this time, dominant cities tended to create territories or *epikráteiai* for themselves, such as the 'empire' of Sybaris, the hinterlands of the great Etruscan centres, and the island dominions of Carthage. Significantly, the figure of Tarquinius Superbus, though he was a 'legitimate' king, is traditionally endowed with characteristics reminiscent of the Greek tyrants, namely, autocracy, violence, ostentation, and so on. Such characteristics must have been common in Etruria also. Indeed, there are singular parallels between the cruelty and impiety displayed by the legendary Mezentius, king of Caere (or indeed by king Thebris or Tybris of Veii), and similar qualities evident in the more or less historical portraits of Phalaris of Agrigentum and Telys of Sybaris. Rome during the later regal era, like the neighbouring cities of Etruria, probably followed the great example of Sybaris in both foreign and domestic politics.

The upheaval and conflict into which Latium was plunged at the very end of the century can be seen as a repercussion of the downfall of the city that had dominated the Mezzogiorno. The fall of Tarquinius, or in other words the traditional ending of the monarchy, coincides with the destruction of Sybaris (though this coincidence may be the work of later annalists, whose speculations have their own interest, and the end of the monarchy should perhaps be dated some few years later). It probably represents an upturn in the fortunes of the party of the 'Servian' reforms, now finding a firmer foundation. However, it signifies neither the eclipse of Etruscan rule in Rome nor the abolition of personal power – though the latter, formerly in the hands of the king, was now exercised by supreme magistrates on a more or less democratic basis (among these was Publius Valerius Publicola, one of the founders of the Roman republic, whose name was recently found in an archaic inscription in the temple of Satricum in Latium).

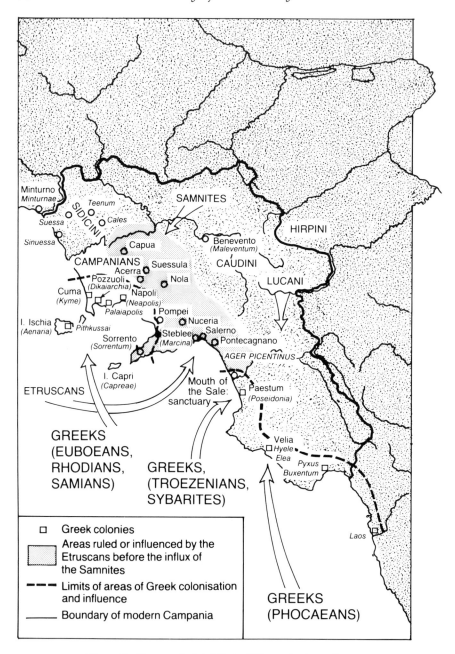

Figure 7 Campania (eighth to fifth centuries BC).

These internal changes were matched by new developments outside Rome. Following his defeat of the grand Etruscan-Italic coalition, the victorious Aristodemus led the forces of the old Greek colony of Cumae in an offensive aimed at the sphere of Etruscan influence, and this helped confirm the new and independent political status of the cities of Latium. Meanwhile in the north there was a show of strength by the inland Etruscan city of Clusium (Chiusi), whose king Lars Porsenna briefly imposed his rule on Rome. Yet his power was never uncontested, and at the battle of Aricia (c. 504 BC) his army, commanded by his son Aruns, was defeated by Aristodemus and the Latins. Cumae continued to dream of dominating the Tyrrhenian region until its tyrant was overthrown by oligarchic opposition around the year 490. Rome now began military and political operations in Latium, which was in turmoil following invasions by the Volscians and the Aequi. A series of 'dictatorships', supported by Etruscan elements, was established. The last and boldest of the 'dictators' was Spurius Cassius, likewise deposed by the oligarchic party after being accused of aspiring to kingship (485 BC).

This outline is enough to indicate that the fortunes of the seafaring cities of Etruria, such as Caere and Vulci, had declined. They had enjoyed their heyday from the seventh to the sixth centuries within the framework of the political and commercial 'balance of power' of the archaic period, which was ultimately based on supremacy of Sybaris. During this last archaic phase, the city of Veii may have attained importance; in the arts, it outshone its neighbour Rome (whose powerful and tenacious enemy it was throughout the fifth century). Falerii, at the centre of a district where a mixed Etruscan-Latin tongue was spoken, may also have flourished, while Tarquinii no doubt profited from its once powerful neighbours' eclipse and regained its early dominance. The Tarquinians set about winning control of substantial territories in the hinterland, to judge by the sudden and brilliant flowering of their tomb-paintings, which must reflect, among other things, considerable economic resources. However, it was above all the more inland and northerly cities of Etruria which rose as the Tyrrhenian coastal centres declined. We have seen that Clusium expanded rapidly under Porsenna, and Volsinii – now Orvieto – also flourished. Moreover, the search for a new and unobstructed route to the sea boosted the fortunes of the Etruscan centres of the

Po valley and the Adriatic, and this process reached its culmination during the fifth century. The internal political situation in the Etruscan cities in the late sixth and early fifth century is not illustrated by much surviving evidence – just a few indirect allusions in Greek and Latin historical tradition, and some local inscriptions. Among the latter, however, are documents of exceptional value, the inscribed gold plaques of Pyrgi. These inform us that in Caere, at some unspecifiable point during the first quarter of the fifth century, power lay in the hands of a single ruler, the man who dedicated the shrine to the Phoenician goddess Astarte. This Thefarie Velianas (or Veliunas), referred to as 'king over Caere' in the Phoenician inscription, is more likely by this time to have been an elective magistrate (*zilac* in the Etruscan inscription): at all events, he seems to have been a tyrant, pursuing a pro-Carthaginian policy.

The Carthaginians, indeed, had benefited from the collapse of the Tyrrhenian commercial and political order underwritten by Sybaris. As the coastal centres of Etruria declined, Carthage found itself free to expand, and this period saw the zenith of its power in the islands and seas of Italy. Its dominion was not unchallenged, however, in the broader strategic and political theatre of the Mediterranean: apart from episodic actions such as that mounted by Dorieus (mentioned above), Massalia (Marseilles) kept a constant watch in the western Mediterranean. At Cape Artemisium, on the Iberian coast, the Carthaginians were defeated by a fleet commanded by 'king' Heracleides of Mylasa (490 BC). It is interesting that this coincided with the battle of Marathon: clearly, the Greek world as a whole now faced the simultaneous threat of two mighty barbarian powers, the Persians in the east and the Carthaginians in the west. The Greeks' enemies may even have consciously recognised and promoted their joint interests. At all events, the fate of the Italian world was linked decisively for the first time to the great issues of the entire Mediterranean arena. The first and most intense phase of this double conflict ended ten years later, in 480 BC, when the Carthaginians were defeated at Himera in Sicily and the Persians at Salamis. The Syracusans won the first battle, and the Athenians the second: these two powers were to exert the greatest external influence on Italian history during the subsequent period.

The heart of archaic Magna Graecia had stopped beating, but

fresh political and cultural vigour was suffusing some of its outlying areas. We have already mentioned the sudden flowering of Cumae in Campania, and other Tyrrhenian centres probably flourished at this time, among them such followers of Sybaris as Posidonia (Paestum) and Velia. Further south, the Straits of Messina were spanned by the creation of a powerful single state ruled by Anaxilas of Reggio and his successors (494–461 BC). But it was Sicily – with the varied and turbulent inheritance of its archaic civilisations – which emerged as the leader of the Hellenic colonies. The power of Syracuse, created by the Deinomenid tyrants Gelon (485–478) and Hiero (478–467), grew rapidly. The Deinomenids initiated a political strategy that unified the Greek elements in Sicily, and put up an obstinate and successful resistance to the pressure of the Carthaginians and their lesser Etruscan allies. Gelon, assisted by Theron, the tyrant of Agrigento, defeated Hamilcar's army at the battle of Himera and drove the Carthaginians back into the easternmost corner of the island, eliminating for many decades the threat they had posed. Shortly afterwards, Hiero defeated an Etruscan fleet in the sea off Cumae (474), opening the way for Syracuse to control the Tyrrhenian. Both these feats of arms had immense consequences throughout the Hellenic world.

These events set the final seal on the history of archaic Italy. A new era, bringing new and different situations and experiences, was about to open.

Plate 1 Bronze Age: a) Vase of the Apennine culture, from Belverde di Cetona (Perugia, Archaeological Museum); b) Mycenaean vase, from Porto Perone (Taranto Archaeological Museum).

Plate 2 Proto-Latial culture. Small cinerary hut-urn, of
terracotta, from Campofattore, Marino (Rome, Museo
Pigorini).

Plate 3 Villanovan culture. Biconical ossuary covered with bronze helmet, from Tarquinii (Florence, Archaeological Museum).

Plate 4 'Oenotrian' culture. Painted geometrical vase, from Sala Consilina (Padula Museum).

Plate 5 Palaeo-Venetic culture. Statuette of warrior, bronze, from Lozzo Atestino (Este, Archaeological Museum).

Plate 6 Gold fibula, 'orientalising' style, from the
Regolini Galassi tomb, Caere, seventh century BC
(Vatican Museum).

Plate 7 Earliest spread of writing in Italy: a) Inscription in Euboean script on vase from Pithecusae, eighth century BC (Ischia Museum); b) Small ivory writing-tablet with 'model' alphabet, from Marsiliana d'Albegna, seventh century BC (Florence, Archaeological Museum).

Plate 8　Evidence of the earliest stages of Greek colonisation in Italy, seventh century BC: a) Fragment of painted vase, Megara Hyblaea (Syracuse Museum); b) Detail of painted bowl bearing the name Aristonothos, from Caere (Rome, Capitoline Museum).

Plate 9 Silver coins from the archaic period, from the major Greek colonies in Italy, sixth century BC. From left to right and top to bottom, Tarentum, Metapontum, Sybaris, Croton, Posidonia.

Plate 10 Architecture of the period of Greek-Tyrrhenian flowering: a) Temples at Posidonia; b) Interior of Etruscan palace reproduced in the Bartoccini tomb of Tarquinii.

Plate 11   Period of Greek-Tyrrhenian flowering: figurative art in the Ionic style: a) Dancers, from the decoration of a temple at the sanctuary of Hera, mouth of the Sele; b) Noble Etruscan family in the painted tomb of the *Baron*, Tarquinii.

Plate 12 Relics of archaic Rome, first half of sixth century BC: a), b) Small lion-shaped ivory plaque with Etruscan inscription, naming Araz Silqetenas Spurianas, from the sanctuary of S. Omobono; c) Detail of the Latin inscription on the cippus of the Lapis Niger in the Roman Forum, with the word *recei* ('king').

Plate 13 Scenes depicting the deeds of the Vibenna brothers and Mastarna, from the François tomb, Vulci (Rome, Villa Albani): a) Caelius Vibenna is freed by his faithful companion Mastarna; b) Slaying of a Roman Tarquin, an enemy of the Vibenna brothers.

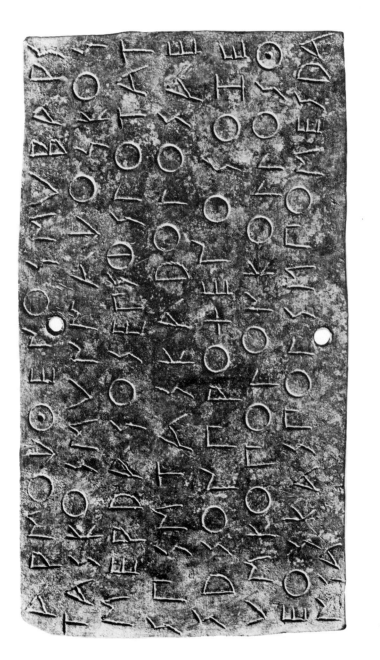

Plate 14 Treaty of alliance between Sybaris and the Serdaioi (Sardinians?), incised on a bronze plaque, sixth century BC, from Olympia (Olympia Museum).

Plate 15 Dedication by the king or lord of Caere, Thefarie Velianas, to the Phoenician goddess Astarte, identified with the Etruscan Uni, on two gold plaques, early fifth century BC, from Pyrgi: a) Text in Phoenician; b) Text in Etruscan.

Plate 16   Naval battle-scenes: a) Painted Etruscan vase, sixth century BC, from Caere (Paris, Louvre); b) Detail of the Etruscan painted vase by the Micali painter, late sixth century BC (London, British Museum).

Plate 17 Etruscan helmet from the naval battle of Cumae, dedicated to Zeus by Hiero of Syracuse, from Olympia (London, British Museum).

Plate 18 Aspects of Etruscan civilisation in the Po valley and the Adriatic region. Decorated bronze situla ('situla della Certosa') late sixth to early fifth century BC, from the necropolis at Bologna (Bologna, Museo Archeologico Civico).

Plate 19 Aspects of Etruscan civilisation in the Po valley and the Adriatic region. Tomb furnishings from the necropolis at Spina, first half of fifth century BC (Ferrara, Archaeological Museum).

Plate 20 Middle Adriatic civilisation. Funerary statue
representing an Italic warrior, sixth century BC, from
Capestrano (Chieti Museum).

Plate 21 Middle Adriatic civilisation. Detail of the cippus of Penne S. Andrea, with a lengthy inscription mentioning the Sabine community (*Safinas tútas*) (Chieti Museum).

Plate 22 Bronze statuette representing a Samnite warrior (Paris, Louvre).

Plate 23   Italic warriors, presumably mercenaries, in a
funerary painting from Paestum (Posidonia), fourth
century BC (Naples, Museo Nazionale).

Plate 24 Gaul, naked and on foot, in combat with a mounted Etruscan: detail of funerary stela from Bologna, late fifth to early fourth century BC (Bologna, Museo Archeologico Civico).

Plate 25   Parade helmets from the fourth century BC: a)
Gallic helmet from a tomb at Caselvatico, Berceto, in the
Tuscan-Emilian   Apennines   (Parma,   Museo   di
Antichità); b) Iapygian helmet from Conversano, Puglia
(Bari Museum).

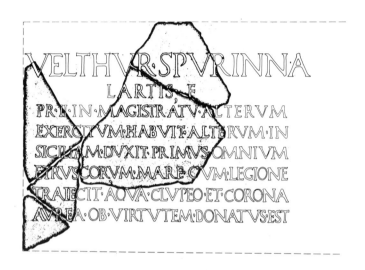

VELTHVR·SPVRINNA
LARTIS·F
PR·I·IN·MAGISTRATV·ALTERVM
EXERCITVM·HABVIT·ALTERVM·IN
SICILIAM·DVXIT·PRIMVS·OMNIVM
ETRVSCORVM·MARE·CVM·LEGIONE
TRAIECIT·AQVA·CLVPEO·ET·CORONA
AVREA·OB·VIRTVTEM·DONATVS·EST

AVLVS·SPVRINNA·VOLTVRIS·F
PR·III·ORGOLNIVM·VELTHVRNENS
CAERITVM·REGEM·IMPERIO·EXPVLIT
ARRETIVM·BELLO·SERVILI·
LATINISNOVEMOPPIDA

Plate 26 Fragmentary Latin inscriptions of the Roman imperial era found at Tarquinii, with records of historical figures of the Spurinna family of Tarquinii: a) Eulogy of Veltur Spurinna; b) Eulogy of Aulus Spurinna.

Plate 27 Defensive fortifications and gateway ('Porta Rosa') in the Greek city of Velia, fourth century BC.

Plate 28 Coinage of the Greek cities of Italy and Greece, fifth and fourth centuries BC. From left to right and top to bottom, didrachm from Cumae, tetradrachm from Reggio, decadrachm from Syracuse from the workshop of Euanetos and dating from the time of Dionysius (face and obverse), tetradrachm of Timoleon (face and obverse), tetradrachm of Agathocles (face and obverse).

Plate 29 Minted and cast coins, from non-Greek cities in Italy, fourth to third centuries BC. From left to right and top to bottom, silver coin from Populonia, as from Volterra (*Velathri*), as from Rome, as from Etruria, as from Todi (*Tutere*), as from Atri (*Hat*), didrachm from Teano (*Tianud*), Roman-Campanian didrachm (*Roma*), bronze coin of the Bruttii (*Brettion*).

Plate 30 War and truce between the Samnites under
M. Fannius and the Romans under Q. Fabius, fragment
of wall painting from a tomb on the Esquiline, early
third century BC (Rome, Capitoline Museum).

Plate 31 Sarcophagus of L. Scipio Barbatus, conqueror of Lucania, with epitaph (Vatican Museum).

Plate 32 Tomb of a noble Etruscan family of the Hellenistic period, belonging to the Pinie family, known as the Giglioli tomb, at Tarquinii.

Plate 33 Coin struck by the Italic peoples during the
Social War, depicting the Italic bull overthrowing the
Roman wolf.

Plate 34 The end of Etruscan civilisation at Perugia: a)
Small urn with ashes of P. Volumnius, inscribed in
Etruscan and Latin, in the tomb of the Volumni; b)
Axonometric drawing of the tomb of the Cutu family,
full of small urns inscribed in Etruscan and Latin, as it
appeared when discovered.

Plate 35   Fragment of Roman marble relief with images of heroes or divinities symbolising the three Etruscan *populi* of Tarquinii, Vulci and Vetulonia (Vatican Museum, formerly Museo Lateranense).

Plate 36 Inscribed cippus with rescript of the Emperor Constantine authorising the inhabitants of Spello to celebrate at home the old religious festivities that took place near Volsinii in Etruria (Spello, Palazzo Comunale).

4

The Age of Crisis
(Fifth to Fourth Century BC)

4

The Age of Crisis
(Fifth to Fourth Centuries BC)

The overall picture: decline of the Greek-Tyrrhenian coastal settlements

Archaeological excavations of the southern Etruscan necropolises reveal the same striking pattern everywhere, though the movement was faster in some places than in others. During the late sixth century and the first half of the fifth century, tombs became less numerous, less imposing, and less richly decorated. A low point was reached during the last decades of the fifth century and first decades of the fourth. In the second half of the fourth century, there was a very marked resurgence in archaeological relics, which then abound for the entire Hellenistic era.

This falling off in the quantity and quality of archaeological evidence, and particularly of finds from tombs (among which Attic pottery has especial significance), is not confined to coastal Etruria. But it is particularly disconcerting there, in both nature and scale, because of the contrasting impression of splendour conveyed by the preceding age, when the immense and ancient burial-grounds of Caere and Vulci had been so richly furnished with precious grave-goods. We find it throughout a wide geographical area. In Rome and Latium, tomb-furnishings had fallen out of use as early as the sixth century: the fact is not easily explained, and may reflect changing social or religious tastes. All the other cities of Magna Graecia, Campania and the Ionian coast, as well as the more or less Hellenised indigenous settlements of the hinterland, appear to match Etruria in their lack of such relics for almost the whole of the fifth century. It is worth noting that a similar scarcity of finds has been recorded at various other western Mediterranean sites, including Carthage itself, though not generally in Sicily.

Certainly this is no matter of appearance or chance. Nor is it due
to local causes. Just because it has the same characteristics over a
wide area, it requires a common historical explanation. Now, in
any age of antiquity the ascertainable archaeological remains
amount to no more than a minute fraction of what the civilisation in
question actually produced, so it follows that when and where
productive activity declines, surviving relics may grow so scarce as
to give the impression of a total void. Other well-known instances
of epochs that are 'non-existent', or virtually so, from an archaeological standpoint include some centuries of the transition between
the Bronze and Iron Ages (the so-called 'Hellenic middle ages', not
confined to Italy), and the European Middle Ages proper. By
analogy, some people refer to a small-scale 'Italic middle ages'.
Given a general economic recession, there are a number of reasons
why the archaeological trail may grow faint or vanish: the
disruption or breaking off of trade, a fall in the standard of living, a
reduction of building works, a lack of innovation in the arts, and
perhaps also some demographic contraction which can make
particular sites appear impoverished. Tradition confirms this
overall picture. At Rome, for instance, where a great many temples
had been dedicated between the sixth and early fifth centuries, the
recorded construction of sacred buildings virtually ceases (the only
exceptions being the temple of Semo Sancus in 466 and that of
Apollo in 433). This is strikingly corroborated by the increasing
scarcity of terracotta revetments throughout the whole Etruscan-
Latin-Campanian region after the first quarter of the fifth century.
The sanctuary at Pyrgi, which must have appeared monumental at
the time of the city's sacking by Dionysius of Syracuse in 384 BC,
had already been given its final form almost a century earlier,
around 470–460, since when no further changes had been made.

We can assert, then, that the coastal societies of southern Italy
and the Tyrrhenian, formerly so prosperous, now entered a period
of decline. This paralleled the rise of the world of classical Greece,
which reached its apogee in the fifth century. In Italy, the mantle of
leadership and progress fell on new shoulders. Fresh forces were
pushing outwards from the interior of the peninsula and appear-
ing from the wider Mediterranean theatre. This marked the
opening of the second phase of Italy's pre-Roman history.

The political-commercial causes that sparked off the crisis have
been referred to in the previous chapter. As the archaic period

closed, the Greek-Tyrrhenian communities of Italy went into irreversible decline. They faced the expansive energies of Greek navigators and colonists in the central and western Mediterranean, the rise of Carthage in Sardinia and Sicily to the point where its power posed a major threat, and the gradual shrinking of the limits of the Etruscans' freedom of navigation in the Tyrrhenian. They were weakened by the conflict between these different forces, the race to seize territorial possessions, and the lack of security on the seas. Finally, such crucial events as the collapse of the Sybaris-based balance of power brought about their demise.

This was a highly sophisticated consumer society, as we can see above all in the artefacts and figurative monuments of the Etruscan cities – though we can imagine a similar culture in some of the Greek cities, as described in the literary sources. At some point, this taste for consumption may have outrun the purchasing power of the citizens' income and accumulated wealth. Etruria's trade with the Greeks and the other Mediterranean powers depended on the extraction of metals from the mines of Vetulonia and Elba, which yielded much exchangeable wealth. These mines may have become less productive, or may have lost their virtual monopoly as other Mediterranean and European mineral resources (in particular, those which the Phocaeans had opened up in Spain) began to be exploited. In Laurion near Athens, silver and zinc mines began production in 483. It is likely that as the purchasing power of Etruria declined, trade grew sluggish along the routes of the Tyrrhenian and the Straits: the well-established exchange of bronze or bronze artefacts from Etruria for Attic pottery dwindled (at this time, the potters of Attica began to look for new markets, starting with the other Etruscan centres on the Adriatic and the Po valley), and all the intermediate ports saw their business fall away. Finally, the crisis may have been exacerbated by domestic political instability and by the social and institutional conflicts that marked the development of the cities, Greek and non-Greek, of the Tyrrhenian coast. Internal unrest would have forced citizens to concern themselves in the first place with purely local problems.

The spread of the eastern Italic peoples

Meanwhile, the privileged status which the coastal centres had for so long enjoyed, and their reputation for power, wealth, and a civilised and brilliant lifestyle, must have aroused the interest of the less culturally advanced population of the Apennine hinterland. From the time when towns first began to form, people were drawn towards places where markets existed and where labour was less strenuous, and this continuous demographic influx may itself have contributed to the process of urban development. Possible confirmation of this is found in the traditions, mentioned above, telling of the Sabines' part in the formation of early Rome, and also in the fact that personal names of eastern Italic origin frequently recur in archaic inscriptions from Etruria and Campania. However, as this movement gradually increased, it must have taken on the character of an organised penetration by linguistic and cultural 'foreigners' who came into conflict with the developed urban societies of the coast. At length, during the fifth and fourth centuries, it was to become a flood submerging much of central and southern Italy.

In considering why and how this happened, we must first of all recall that a group of Italic peoples of Oscan-Umbrian linguistic stock had established a fairly stable culture from the beginning of the archaic period. This relatively advanced civilisation, called 'Picenian', was centred on the Adriatic coast: today, inscriptional evidence allows us to attribute it confidently to the Sabines. It was not significantly involved in the great ethnic movements. However, other Sabine peoples living in the mountainous Apennine regions, and those who descended from them, enjoyed a much less settled and developed style of life, and it is to them that we can look for the origins of the migratory impulse. As the population increased, the need for larger territories must have stimulated more or less abrupt incursions into the relatively hospitable lands of the upper Apennine valleys. From there, further movements must have taken place, which took on a religious and martial aspect through the venerable ritual formula of the *ver sacrum* or 'sacred spring': the young men of a given generation armed themselves, so tradition tells us, and emigrated, in an act of expiation enjoined by the gods. This was a development of the greatest importance, a cultural mutation whose consequences were incalculable. Perhaps it represented a continuation of the great prehistoric movement from east to west across the Adriatic and the peninsula.

The historian, however, must look for concrete causes. What impelled the mountain-dwellers of the Apennines to awaken all of a sudden from the somnolent tradition of centuries, with its pastoral economy, relatively constant and modest population, tribal conservatism and cultural inertia? One catalyst must surely have been the contacts established between the inland peoples, with their potential for development, and the evolving civilisation of the western Italian coast. There must have been a response – indeed, a kind of chain reaction – tending to redress the inequalities in mental habits, social structure and style of life between districts not so very distant from one another: Aquae Cutiliae, for instance, in the Rieti basin, the legendary birthplace of the Sabines, was less than 100 km (60 miles) by road from Rome, while the Samnite sanctuary of the goddess Mefitis was similarly close to the Greek sanctuary of Hera at the mouth of the Sele.

The demand for agricultural and craft workers, as well as for troops, may have helped bring the two worlds closer together and establish their mutual relations. This kind of dialectic recurs in the history of civilisation. On one hand, there are fully developed societies destined to some degree of decline: on the other, there are fresh forces pressing in on the frontier, ready to take their place. During the period of the great Mediterranean struggles of the fourth and third centuries, the eastern Italic peoples were to figure largely as mercenaries under the ensign of the warrior-god Mars or Mamars. Enlistment as mercenaries must have played some part in the earliest phase of their expansion, though it may at first have been inextricably bound up with the whole relationship of alliance or *symmachía* between the Greek-Tyrrhenian cities and the indigenous inland peoples. This is how we should understand not only (and obviously) the relations between the colonies – especially Sybaris – of Magna Graecia and the hinterland, but also the records telling us that Umbrians and Daunians took part in the Etruscan attack on Cumae in 524 BC. Soldiers of Italic origin may already have figured among the mercenaries in the pay of the Deinomenids in Syracuse. Mercenaries from Campania, Samnites settled in that region, were certainly sent by Neapolis to help the Athenians in their struggle with Syracuse. Immigrants, whether they come as individuals, in groups, or en masse, tend to establish stable occupancy of new lands. Once consolidated, they move on to further occupation and conquest. Private or semi-private

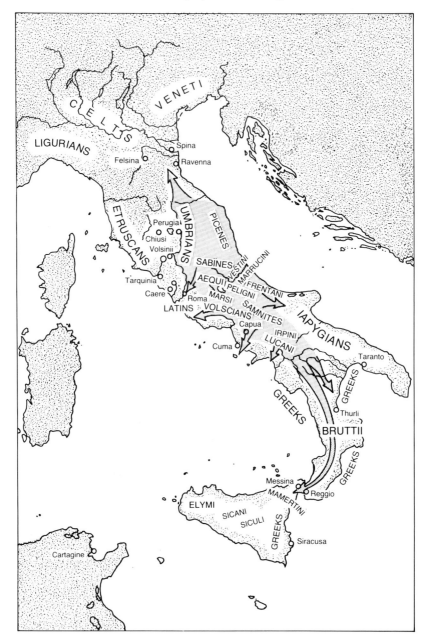

Figure 8 Spread and distribution of Oscan-Umbrian-speaking eastern Italic peoples.

initiatives, still within the old framework of political sovereignty, probably gave way very gradually to a 'capture of power' by the immigrant peoples, who then created new forms of state organisation and followed the path of aggressive outward expansion.

We know that the inland peoples first broke through towards the Tyrrhenian coast in that part of Latium which lies between the Alban Hills and the valley of the Liris. This ethnic and political borderland was almost without seafaring settlements and major urban centres, and its condition was rather backward, especially in comparison with the Monti Aurunci and Monti Ausoni. At the end of the archaic period, it had been much weakened by a number of factors – the loosening of Etruscan control over both sea and land, the Latins' aspirations towards autonomy, the conflict between Etruria and Cumae, and the effects of the struggle for supremacy at Rome. Between the late sixth and mid-fifth centuries, the resulting power vacuum opened the way for incursions by the Oscan-Umbrian-speaking peoples who had lived since early times among the ridges of the Monti Sabini, the Monti Simbruini and the Monti Ernici, and the valleys lying behind them. There has been much scholarly perplexity and controversy over the origins and dialects of these peoples, known as the Sabines, the Hernici, the Aequi and the Volscians: were they of ancient Sabellian stock, or did they belong to the more northerly Umbrian branch (as seems to be the case with the Volscians)? At all events, they represented the earliest and furthest westward advance of the eastern Italic peoples. Well into the historic period, some Sabines, perhaps following in the footsteps of their early Iron Age ancestors or namesakes, took their place in the Roman community when Attus Clausus (in a typical episode of semi-private immigration) settled a group of his followers in the city at the end of the sixth century. In 468, Appius Herdonius took the Sabines to the verge of seizing possession of the city (a case, now, of military conquest from outside), and they subsequently established themselves in the sanctuary of Lucus Feroniae on the right bank of the Tiber, perhaps succeeding in occupying or controlling part of the Faliscan territory, whose language they significantly altered. The Volscians spread out over Latium as far as the sea-coast, occupying Velitrae, Satricum, Antium (Anzio), Terracina, Fondi and Formia. They created a well-organised and effective political system which must have absorbed many cultural and organisational features of the old coastal civilisation (though up to now no clear archaeological profile has emerged of it). Together with the Aequi, they were to constitute a standing threat to the very existence of the surviving Latin communities, and of Rome, for several decades from the early fifth century until 430.

During this phase of their expansion, these eastern Italic peoples of the Umbrian branch, having worked their way up the Tiber valley and finding their path westward blocked by the un-conquerable frontier settlements of Etruria such as Volsinii (modern Orvieto), Clusium (Chiusi), Perugia, Cortona and Arezzo, may well have begun consolidating and extending their occupation of the region known historically as Umbria, particularly the valleys of the Topino and the Chiascio and their tributaries. They would have acquired elements of urban culture and Etruscanised manners and habits – in the first place, writing. Among the evidence for such a view is the flourishing of Tuder (Todi), whose name became a byword for a 'border town'; the birth of Plestia at Colfiorito, whose name features on the earliest surviving Umbrian inscription, recently come to light; and prob-ably also the foundation of Iguvium (Gubbio) by people originating from Attidium, as recorded in the tradition set down, rather later, in the Iguvine Tables. Here in the strange land of Gubbio they found themselves surrounded by threats from unknown peoples such as the Etruscans themselves (Turskus), those who dwelt towards the Adriatic (Iapuzkus), and the 'Nerini' (Naharkus), who are difficult to identify (perhaps these 'Naharkus' were other eastern Italic people speaking a non-Umbrian language, pressing in from the south?). We should accept the traditional account – echoed in certain passages of Strabo (V 1, 7 and 10; 2, 1 and 9–10) – that this wave of expansion spread onwards, even before the Gallic invasion and in competition with Etruscan supremacy, to reach as far as Romagna and the Adriatic coast, where the Umbrians occupied Sarsina, Rimini and Ravenna. Striking and now certain archaeological confirmation of this has been found, above all in the burial-grounds of the Imola region and the Lamone and Savio valleys.

The other front of the eastern Italic region, looking to the south and inhabited by Oscan-speaking peoples, presumably suffered this migratory restlessness by the beginning of the fifth century, if not earlier. However, only in the second half of the century were its inhabitants able to embark on their momentous and irresistible advance. It is very probable that they were at first held in check by the density of Greek colonial settlement and by the organised nature of the indigenous societies of the hinterland, which were economically and culturally oriented towards the colonies. Archaeological evidence of the indigenous strongholds is now coming to light, especially in Lucania. The flourishing Apulian peoples may also have stood in their way. However, although it is unlikely to have taken place in early times or on a massive scale (as some have maintained), eastern Italic infiltration into the southern part of the peninsula perhaps took place as early as the archaic period. This is indicated by both place-names and archaeology (there are, for instance, certain similarities between the culture of the upper Sele valley and that of the middle Adriatic region).

All the Italic peoples who migrated into southern Italy were descended from the Samnites of the Molise and Hirpinia regions, and they in turn were traditionally held to be akin to the Sabines, whose name they shared (the Oscan *Safinim* is equivalent to *Samnium*: the form *Samnites* is derived from *Samnium*). Samnites gradually made their way into the plain of Campania, probably rousing the local indigenous peoples to activity as they did so. In 430 BC, this led to the establishment of the Campanian people, with Capua as their organisational centre, and to the end of Etruscan domination. Shortly afterwards, Cumae fell, and with it the whole Greek colonial system (at Neapolis, a kind of Greek-Samnite condominium was formed, with magistrates of both races). The Campanians were also known as Oscans (Osci), and the tongues spoken by the eastern Italic peoples who lived in the south are known generally as the Oscan language. The Samnites were the forebears, too, of the Lucani, who moved into the Tyrrhenian coasts of southern Italy below the Sorrento peninsula between the late fifth and early fourth centuries, and then across as far as the Ionian coast. The Lucani in turn gave rise to Bruttii or Bruttians (known in Italian as the *Bruzi*, and called *Brettioi* by the Greeks), who spread into what is now Calabria. Finally, as we shall see, a far-flung eastern Italic outpost, settled by mercenaries, took root in Messina in Sicily.

Other movements of inland peoples: Iapygians, Sicels, Gauls

The widespread restlessness and aggressiveness of the inland
peoples at this time has broad historical causes. It was not confined
to the Oscan-Umbrian-speaking Apennine peoples (as if prompted
by their special needs or characteristics), but manifested itself
simultaneously, though on a smaller scale, among other indigenous peoples. In the south of the peninsula, the most important
group, with the most clearly marked individual character and
cultural personality, was the Iapygians (*Iapyges*) or Apulians
(*Apuli*). They lived in the south-east, in modern Italy's Puglia
province, still usually called Apulia in English. The Iapygians were
traditionally subdivided into the Daunians (centred on Foggia), the
Peucetians (in the Bari region) and the Messapians (in the Salento
peninsula). Even if we ignore the tales about their origins,
archaeological evidence indicates that they tended to push westwards towards the Tyrrhenian. In the archaic period Apulian
geometric pottery is already widespread and its influence is
perceptible in Lucania and indeed in Campania and Etruria. The
Daunians were mentioned among the participants in the great
Etruscan war against Cumae, in the second half of the sixth
century, and Callimachus refers (in the *Aitia*) to an attack on Rome
by the Peucetians, which we cannot date with any precision but
which was perhaps earlier than has hitherto been suspected. It is of
little importance that each of these traditions may record the
activities of mercenaries, rather than independent military
campaigns. At the beginning of the fifth century, the stubborn
resistance the Iapygians had mounted against Greek political and
cultural penetration took on a more turbulent and menacing
aspect. There was a series of border wars – commemorated by
votive gifts left by the Tarentines at Delphi – before Tarentum, in
alliance with Reggio, suffered a bloody defeat in 473 BC. *Pace*
modern historians, there may be some truth in the account given
by Diodorus Siculus (XI, 32) which tells how the victorious
Iapygians then actually embarked on a punitive expedition,
crossing the whole of Magna Graecia and reaching Reggio. (Its
ruler Mikythos, the successor of Anaxilas, subsequently tried – for
defensive reasons or from motives of prestige – to set up a short-
lived military colony at Pyxous on the Lucanian frontier.) Further
Apulian expansion remained an unrealised historical possibility. It

was blocked by the highly organised territorial structure of the Greek colonies and by the beginnings of the southward offensive which the eastern Italic peoples from further north were now mounting. However, evidence from later decades shows that these south-eastern Italic people continued to entertain forceful and enterprising strategic objectives embracing the entire southern area of the peninsula: witness the alliance against Tarentum between Brindisi and the pan-Hellenic colony of Thurii (c. 440), and the offer of assistance which the Messapian king Artas made to the Athenians when they were fighting Syracuse. Here we see advance notice of the major military and political role the Messapians played in the affairs of Magna Graecia a century later – admittedly under very different conditions.

Outside the peninsula, the Siculan *condottiere* Ducetius similarly exploited the internal strife and mutual rivalry of the Greek cities in order, initially, to create a large indigenous state in the heart of Sicily (460–451 BC). Defeated by the Syracusans and exiled to Corinth, he later returned, founding the colony of Calacte with the consent of both Greeks and indigenous peoples and with the support of Syracuse itself (446). He was partly inspired by rebellious feelings among the descendants of the original inhabitants, resentful of the colonial world; and particular motifs of local tradition must have played a part. His capital, Palice, was established near the site of one of the most venerated Siculan holy places, not far from modern Palagonia. But the resistance of the Hellenised or semi-Hellenised communities of the hinterland to the dominance of the great coastal cities was probably a more significant factor. At all events, Ducetius' strategy, which soon came to follow purely personal ends, by no means reversed the trend of Sicilian history, for it eventually reinforced the supremacy of Syracuse.

We must turn, finally, to a phenomenon of wider scope and implications, in which northern Italy was caught up in the interplay of pan-European forces and reactions, namely, the Celtic invasion. Its context is the general restlessness affecting the Italian interior, the familiar pattern of semi-barbarian peoples drawn from inland regions towards more civilised areas – whether attracted by the flourishing settlements near at hand in the Po valley and along the Adriatic, or by the more distant glamour of the Greek-

Tyrrhenian world of the peninsula. The Gauls (the Roman term is interchangeable with the Greek 'Celts'), however, differed from the other peoples mentioned above in that they came from outside Italy. They belonged, in fact, to a large ethnic group inhabiting central and western Europe. It is generally held that around the fifth century the Celtic world expanded dramatically, especially towards the south – specifically into Italy and the Balkans. But there are now strong reasons for believing that they penetrated Italy considerably earlier, beginning – as Livy states (V, 34 and 35: his account was formerly rejected as anachronistic) – in the late seventh and early sixth centuries, when Tarquinius Priscus reigned at Rome and Massalia (Marseilles) was founded. The ethnic origins of the Celts may even lie in an area including the Alpine and sub-Alpine slopes of Italy – witness the supposedly proto-Celtic character of the Lepontine inscriptions (produced by the Lepontii who lived in the lacustrine areas of Lombardy). In any case, we must envisage the Celtic invasions of Italy not as a single catastrophic event but as a series of over-lapping southward expansions, in which the later arrivals pushed furthest. From the account in Livy and the description in Polybius (II, 17 ff.), we can locate the Insubres at the heart of present-day Lombardy, centred on Mediolanum (Milan); the Cenomani in the region of Brescia and Verona; the Salluvii around the Ticino, north-west of the Insubres, and the Boii and Lingones in Emilia and Romagna; and the Senones along the Adriatic shoreline as far as the modern Marches. A crucial moment must have been the crossing of the Po, an action that directly threatened the Etruscan territories of that district. Further key events must have included the entry of the Gauls, principally the Senones, into the peninsula, which came in the late fifth and early fourth centuries with attacks on Tyrrhenian Etruria, Rome (burnt by Gauls shortly after 390 BC) and Apulia.

The Gauls' primitive and savage customs, vividly described by Diodorus Siculus (V. 26 ff.), must have made a deep impression on the classical world: here, plainly, was a people at a very different level of culture from the civilised Greeks and Etruscans. The two worlds became implacably opposed. The Gauls typically moved in a series of bold and rapid thrusts or raids, avoiding the cities in their incursions; only in northern Italy and the Marches did they establish lasting territorial control and farm the land. This fitful and uneven pattern of advance explains why we find the Gauls in the

Figure 9 The expansion and distribution of the Gauls.

peninsula, in Etruria, in Rome and even in Apulia by the beginning of the fourth century, even though it was not until the middle of the same century that a stable Celtic presence took root in Emilia (at Bologna, which was to take the name Bononia, probably after the Boii, and at Marzabotto). The Celts went on to play an active and developing role in the subsequent history of Italy as a whole.

'Peripheral' developments and 'outside' influences: Greek-Tyrrhenian Italy and Syracusan and Athenian policies in the fifth century

The notion of an 'Italic middle ages', while it may be valid overall, does not apply everywhere in the historical arena of the 'Italian region' in the broad sense. We have noted that the vital centres of the Greek colonial world were displaced to the margins of Magna Graecia, and the same seems to have happened to the whole political and cultural heritage of the Greek-Tyrrhenian coastal strip. The crisis that overtook the long-established and glorious cities of the Ionian and Tyrrhenian seas during the fifth century was counterbalanced by a flowering of the outlying territories. They seem to have adopted the traditions of Hellenic Italy and Etruria and kept the torch of civilisation alight. Inland Etruria and the Etruscan Po valley assumed the role of maritime Etruria, and Sicily replaced Magna Graecia. The outward sign of this shift lies in the great abundance of Attic pottery of classical style found respectively at Spina and in the cities of Greek Sicily, dating from the very period at which such artefacts thin out or disappear in the Tyrrhenian settlements and the southern Italian mainland.

It is in fact archaeological evidence that chiefly suggests that the Etruscan cities of the interior grew rapidly and decisively. Some, such as Clusium and Fiesole, were of course already important during the archaic period; and not all the coastal cities lost all their traditional greatness, or lost it at a stroke. We know that Tarquinii enjoyed a marked revival at the close of archaic times, probably becoming dominant in southern Etruria. The fact that the funerary art of Tarquinii continues well into the fifth century, with an abundance of monuments and a high aesthetic standard, may show that here, in particular, crisis and recession were resisted, allowing the city to retain the territorial pre-eminence and the political-military, cultural and religious prestige which we know it had at the time of its wars with Rome. However, the most telling indications of a lively artistic production under the influence of classical Greece, and thus of a period of especial vigour during the fifth or fifth and fourth centuries, are found elsewhere – at Veii, Falerii, Volsinii (Orvieto) (votive figures and architectural terracottas), at Clusium (funerary sculpture and painting) and at Cortona and Arezzo (bronze statues and utensils). These data must be related to what was presumably a general shift of economic and political interests from the coasts to the thoroughfares of the interior, which followed the lakes and rivers with which Etruria is well endowed. In particular, an important axis of communication and trade established itself along the Tiber valley (perhaps also involving Latin, Sabine and Umbrian communities). Besides the early record of Porsenna's campaigns, there is evidence of the dominance of Clusium in the central region, which may have paralleled Tarquinii's hegemony to the south. Above all, it was probably during this period that the association or confederation of the twelve (later fifteen) great Etruscan states, both coastal and inland, was properly established. These can be identified with some certainty as Caere, Tarquinii, Vulci, Roselle, Vetulonia, Populonia, Veii, Volsinii, Clusium, Perugia, Cortona, Arezzo, Fiesole and Volterra. They were organised through their annual 'congress' (*conventus*) at the sanctuary of the god Voltumna (Fanum Voltumnae) near Volsinii (Orvieto). Primarily religious and economic, this association also had political and military aspects. In time, Volsinii itself also became a very important centre, even being dubbed 'capital of Etruria' (Valerius Maximus, IX 1) – a title justified archaeologically by the splendour of the Orvieto necropolises.

Another larger and more fertile territory in which development took place was the Etruscan-dominated region lying beyond the Tuscan-Emilian Apennines. As naval activity in the Tyrrhenian became increasingly obstructed, so the strategic needs of international trade were met by the alternative Adriatic route. In time, the old communities of Etruria drew new life from the Adriatic ports. The question of earlier Etruscan presence in the Po valley is beset with problems, but certainly between the late sixth and early fifth centuries, and no sooner, the great settlements of Emilia and Romagna rose to prominence – Felsina-Bologna and Marzabotto in the interior, and such coastal centres as Adria (on the frontier of Venetic territory), Spina, and probably Ravenna and Rimini. Foremost in importance was the port of Spina at the mouth of the old southerly branch of the Po. Celebrated by the ancients, Spina was so receptive to Greek influence that it was believed to have been founded by the Pelasgians and was known as *polis Hellenis*. With its rich necropolises, it has yielded an abundant harvest of Attic vases. From the historical sources, and also – though tentatively – from archaeological data, we can infer that Etruscan control or influence in northern Italy must have extended, at least for a while, to western Emilia, from Modena to Piacenza, and north of the Po to Mantua, which has an Etruscan name, if not further. There is greater doubt about the Ligurian region: here if anywhere, contacts by sea along the Tyrrhenian were involved, with strategic outposts north of the mouth of the Arno, where the ethnically mixed port of Pisa rose and flourished, and perhaps also a few coastal trading posts. Along the Adriatic, the Etruscans may possibly have made their presence felt even south of Romagna. Strabo (V, 4, 2) tells us that the sanctuary of Cupra in the Piceno region was founded by Tyrrhenians.

Northern Etruria as a whole from the fifth to the early fourth century was an area of intense and dynamic civilisation, at a level of development unprecedented in northern Italy. This acted as a spur to the development of the local peoples: the Venetic inhabitants of the middle and upper reaches of the Po who produced what is known as the Golasecca culture, and the Alpine dwellers. They acquired writing from the Etruscans. The Etruscans in their turn absorbed local elements, and spread Italic artefacts and the fame of Italic culture through their very wide-ranging contacts, which stretched beyond the Alps towards central and northern Europe. Their prosperity may have been short-lived – it was soon undermined by the incursions of the Umbrians from the south and the Gauls from the north and west, as well as by natural causes (the port of Spina was already backward and silted up in the fourth century, and Adria had taken over) – but it was thanks to them that the upper Adriatic was opened up once for all to the great movements of civilisation and the play of Mediterranean commercial and political interests.

Historical sources and archaeological data also confirm that the fortunes of the old colonies of Magna Graecia were stagnant or declining. This applied particularly to the 'central' part of the Gulf of Taranto, though not to Tarentum itself at the northern limit or to the more southerly centres (situated in modern Calabria) of Croton, Locri and Reggio. Locri enjoyed an especially brilliant cultural and artistic flowering in the first half of the fifth century, and Reggio became in some ways the leading centre at the time of the 'Kingdom of the Straits' created by Anaxilas. However, the political initiative and the traditions and inheritance of Greek power in Italy were soon to move outside the peninsula, passing entirely to Syracuse. Having repulsed the Carthaginian threat at Himera and put an end to the Etruscans' remaining naval pretensions off Cumae, the Syracusans found themselves able to take total and unimpeded control of the seas of Italy. The two major Greek territories which might to some extent have rivalled Syracuse in Sicily and on the adjacent Italian coast, Agrigento-Himera and Reggio-Messina, were gradually subsumed within the 'Empire' of the Deinomenids. Even though the full fruits of this opportunity could not be harvested as early as the first half of the fifth century – as they were to be a few decades later under the impetuous and brilliant political leadership of Dionysius – Syracuse lost no time in imposing its own programme of action and self-advancement on Italy 'from outside', taking over some aspects of Carthage's role. With its naval base on Ischia, Syracuse established firm supremacy on the coast of Campania, still the key to Tyrrhenian Italy. There followed an attempted offensive against Etruria itself, directed especially against the old mining centres of the north. The admirals Phayllus and Apelles led two consecutive naval expeditions, which laid waste stretches of the Etruscan, Elban and Corsican coast and occupied them temporarily (454–453 BC). However, these campaigns proved inconclusive, partly because of disputes between the commanders which were to lead to the trial of Phayllus.

Meanwhile, Athens was another and novel force impinging during this same period – and from further afield – on the Italian political and strategic theatre. From the earliest times, the cultural prestige of Athens had exerted itself indirectly, as shown (other indications apart) by the vast quantity of pottery imported from Attica, while its economic prestige is attested by the growing importance of Attic coinage in monetary exchange, revealed by excavations of money-hoards. In the aftermath of the Persian wars,

Athens was at the zenith of its power, and began to turn its attention westwards towards the Italian area, first with Themistocles and then, decisively, with Pericles. All the surviving accounts suggest that Athenian imperialism began by establishing discreet contacts. After gaining fuller knowledge of the situation, Athens would proceed to set up a network of friendly relations (some of which are documented, while others must be assumed) with the various centres and settlements that had remained on the margins of Syracuse's dominion, or which resented or opposed Syracusan supremacy. These comprised Reggio and Locri, the Etruscans, Latins and Apulians, and probably Carthage itself. By establishing a quasi-colonial protectorate over Neapolis (453 BC), Athens replaced Syracuse as possessor of the naval base on Ischia and potential controller of Campania. Around the same time, new life was breathed into the old dream of a renaissance in the fortunes of Sybaris, ruined nearly seventy years earlier. After a series of trials and errors, Lampon, deeply versed in Italian politics and strategy, led an Athenian expedition which helped re-establish the ancient city (446–444), now in an entirely new form and with the new name of Thurii. It was to be a colony of all the Hellenes, boasting an orderly and democratic legal code and a town-plan strictly laid down on 'Hippodamian' lines. The classical spirit, its rationality and its entire ethos, seem as clearly expressed in this almost Utopian foundation as they do in the figures on the Parthenon, completed at the same period. The city faced many threats and problems. It had its own internal tensions and contradictions (the Doric party soon gained the upper hand over the Ionians, and a rift opened up between the supporters of Athens and those of Sparta). The old colonies were hostile – in particular Tarentum, which set up a competing neo-colony of its own, Heraclea, which was near the site of Siris, another famous ruin. Finally, the invading eastern Italic peoples, the Lucanians and the Bruttians, were pressing down threateningly from the interior. But Thurii took root and survived.

The real aim of this lengthy preparatory phase of Athenian involvement in Italy was to gain dominion over Sicily. In pursuit of this, it seemed particularly useful to form links of mutual support with colonies originally founded by Euboeans – who were Ionians, like the Athenians, and thus inclined to be hostile to Doric Syracuse. This meant Reggio and then also – in Sicily itself and very near Syracuse – Leontinoi. With the outbreak of the Peloponnesian War and the death of Pericles, this strategy was adapted to the new struggle. Between 427 and 425, three Athenian naval expeditions embarked against Syracuse, all failing for a variety of reasons – including, ultimately, the assertion of a true sense of Siceliote (Sicilian Greek) 'nationalism' in the Gela accords (424). The culminating expression of Athenian imperialist ambitions in the west was the famous Sicilian campaign of Alcibiades, backed by all the resources of the Athenian democracy (415–413). In this campaign, a part, though not a decisive one, was played by Athens' allies among the Italian city-states. Soldiers from Campania and even ships from Etruria were involved, as were the Euobean colonies in Sicily, some of the Sicels, and the Elymi from western Sicily, who were flourishing at this time (and whose capital, Segesta, had been attacked by Selinus: this was the immediate cause of the war). However, the episode as a whole affected Italic interests only marginally. Its real context – and here its importance was dramatic and decisive – is Greek history, at the decisive moment of the duel between Athens and Sparta. The defeat at Syracuse of the attackers' 'grand armada', following a hard-fought battle in which the Spartans directly aided the defence, sounded the moral and material death-knell to the age of Athenian supremacy. Syracuse emerged from the struggle with new strength, ready, once further threats and mishaps had been overcome, to take on with renewed vigour the role of a dominating or controlling power in mainland Italy.

If we now consider the situation in the Greek-Tyrrhenian world generally, we can say that the history of its decline, and of the power struggles that rent Italy during the fifth century, was interwoven with the history of social developments and political forms. The rule of tyrants, which had been so widespread at the close of the archaic period, was no more than a phase, though a clearly-marked one, in the evolution of the western *polis*, and it tended to disappear as the new era dawned. Here and there, however, it persisted, establishing itself in the form of dynastic rule and becoming identified with the fortunes of the state itself. (It is significant that this happened in Reggio and Syracuse, the areas of furthermost Italy and of Sicily which showed the greatest historical vitality at this period.) In many cities of Magna Graecia – Croton, Locri, Reggio, Cumae – and probably in some non-Greek cities too, tyrannies were replaced by oligarchies which claimed power or enjoyed a restoration in the full sense of the term. In Rome, Spurius Cassius, thought to have aspired after absolute power, fell, and the patrician regime of the Fabii took firm hold (485 to 461 BC). Similar developments surely took place in Etruria (where aristocratic governments had in general lasted longer): it was perhaps at this period that both Rome and Etruria acquired that fear and hatred of kings and tyrants so characteristic of them, which became one of the basic themes and expressions of republican ideology. In some cases, however, as at Tarentum and Syracuse, the fall of tyrants led directly to the establishment of democratic regimes. Undoubtedly, the Athenian presence in Italy was a determining influence in the process of democratisation affecting the Italian *poleis*. Around the middle of the fifth century, virtually every city in the Greek-Tyrrhenian world attempted democratic innovations and renewed its constitution and laws. The aim was to achieve some ideal conception of the state, but the cities failed (partly because of their internal instability) to regain their old prosperity. Among relevant episodes were the gains made by the plebeians at Rome and the legal proclamation there of the Twelve Tables, which was declared to be of Athenian inspiration.

Another marked characteristic of this period, also considerably influenced by Athenian contacts with Italy, was the spread of the classical spirit. This is seen especially in the artistic creations of Magna Graecia, but it also affected the non-Greek Tyrrhenian region. At the same time, the aftermath of the Persian war saw the drawing of an ever more marked distinction between Greeks and barbarians. In Italy, this led to a weakening of the sense of unity that had bound together the old Greek-Tyrrhenian *koiné*. Moreover, the Italic world, especially Etruria, seems to have been unable to keep up with the great intellectual and artistic strides classical Greece and its colonies were taking. The civilisation of the Etruscan and Italic world as a whole remained relatively backward. Its character become provincial; it shared in common experiences and innovations only as a more or less passive imitator. And this situation was to last until the end of Italy's pre-Roman history.

Figure 10 Overall distribution of peoples and principal places
of Italy between the fifth and third centuries BC.

Italy and the wars of the fourth century

These, then, were the elements old and new which were mixed together and shaken up in the crucible of fourth-century Italy. An era of crisis now opened for Italy. The ancient communities and cultures continued to decline, new forces took still uncertain shape, different ethnic groups clashed and clashed again, and bloody wars broke out. But fresh forces were laying the foundations for a new and more stable dispensation, and in culture and the arts the influence of late classical Greece brought about signs of renovation.

For a preliminary overall view of the chief aspects and trends of these decades, and as a guide to the somewhat confused course of events, let us focus on the following points:

1. The old organisation centred on the city-state, typical of the archaic period, together with the balance of power associated with it, was a thing of the past. In its place we find on the one hand a growing tendency for particular cities or individual *condottieri* to impose hegemonic or imperial rule, and on the other hand the coming together of cities in political leagues intended to overcome the weakness of their isolation and allow them to act in common. The fourth century in Italy was indeed the age of leagues. The system, in part imitated from Greek models, first appeared in Magna Graecia and Etruria, and was then copied by the Oscan-speaking Italic peoples (Samnites and Lucanians).

2. As the sense of a common Greek-Tyrrhenian civilisation weakened further, the Greek colonies of Magna Graecia (the Italiotes) and of Sicily (Siceliotes) seem to have felt a renewed awareness of their originally and fundamentally Greek nature. Close ties were renewed between colonies and their mother-cities (Syracuse and Corinth, Tarentum and Sparta). By seeking aid from the mother country, the colonies brought a new, external factor into the power struggles of the Italic world.

3. The 'new arrivals' – eastern Italic peoples and Gauls – altered the whole fabric of the old Italy. But they remained confined to areas and ways of life that were unsettled, precarious and conflict-ridden by comparison to the older-established cities (except perhaps in Campania, a region that particularly favoured meeting and mingling). They did, however, create at least two solid

political and territorial enclaves: the area of the Samnites in the peninsular Mezzogiorno, and that of the Gauls in northern Italy (this latter region was to take its name from them, being known as Gallia into the Roman era).

4. A new factor began to affect this complex interaction, above all in the second half of the century. This unexpected and (so to speak) silent development was the political and military growth of Rome. It eventually brought to an end this era, and indeed the whole cycle of Italic history (as we shall see in the next chapter), but for the moment it was just one component of the general picture.

5. Carthaginian imperialism was an ever-present, though often latent, danger on the margins. It had no more than an indirect influence on events in Italy, at least during the period under discussion.

Two salient features characterised the first decades of the fourth century. On the one hand, the Gauls reached the limit of their aggressive advance into the peninsula, as did the Lucanians to the south. On the other hand, Dionysius of Syracuse embarked on a strategy of expansion in Italy and along its coastline. A great general and statesman, Dionysius began his successful career by confronting and rebutting the dangerously reactivated forces of the Carthaginians, who had threatened the final and complete subjugation of Sicily. He was hailed as chief, with the title of Archon, by almost the entire Greek community of the island he had saved (392 BC). Dionysius pursued to its limit the ideal of power that had been the motif of Syracusan history during the fifth century. Secure in his dominion over most of Sicily, he turned towards Italy. He took on and defeated the league of the Italiotes, headed by Reggio. In this he was assisted by the Lucanians who by this time (386) were already pressing in on the Greek colonies. Reggio was captured and laid waste, and the entire western extremity of the peninsula came under Syracusan rule. In the years that followed, Dionysius set in motion an even more wide-ranging strategic plan. Naval actions were undertaken along the coasts of both the Adriatic and the Tyrrhenian. His aim seemed to be to grip the whole Italian peninsula in a vice and extend Syracusan control as far as possible. Several settlements (connected with Dionysius' interest in Epirus) were founded along the east coast of the Adriatic. Ancona and Adria were other new colonies – the latter being, as we have seen, an old Venetic-Etruscan port. In the Tyrrhenian, a sixty-trireme force from Syracuse sacked the sanctuary of Pyrgi, the port of Caere (384). This expedition may have been aimed at the mining areas, and perhaps founded a 'Syracusan port' in Corsica.

These undertakings were influenced, and favoured, by events within the peninsula. At the time of Dionysius' rise to power, the Romans conquered Veii and the Gauls were making inroads into Etruria, attacking Rome (which they burned around 386) and reaching as far as Apulia. Also at this period, somewhere in central Italy (the exact site has not been traced), the Gauls suffered a defeat at the hands of the Caerites. The ascendancy of Syracuse brought about a new set of alliances, for the traditional hostility between Syracusans and Etruscans, and the conflicts between Etruria and the Gauls, favoured a rapprochement between Dionysius and the Gauls. This may seem surprising, given the distance and the differences separating the two parties, but it is understandable, for Syracusans and Gauls had probably made contact in Apulia, in the Marches and especially in the northern Italian coastal area. Here, the basis for an anti-Etruscan *entente* was perhaps more obvious. So far as the Tyrrhenian coast is concerned, Dionysius' decision to attack Etruria may have owed something to the threat on the other flank posed by the Gallic bands which had penetrated Etruscan territory and conquered Rome. It is also possible that at this time Gallic mercenaries made their appearance in the Syracusan armies.

The outbreak of fresh hostilities with Carthage in 383 had considerable repercussions in Italy. The Greek cities of what is now Calabria renewed their resistance to Syracuse, with the aid of both the Carthaginians and the Lucanians. Dionysius occupied Croton, but the struggle dragged on in both Italy and Sicily until peace was concluded in 374. Southern Italy was now divided into a zone of well-established Syracusan influence and another and larger territory controlled by a new Italiote league comprising Tarentum, Metapontum, Heraclea and Thurii. Tarentum, governed by the Pythagorean sage Archytas, was the chief city.

Dionysius turned his political and military attention, particularly during his last years, away from Italy and towards Greece. He supported Sparta, an old and faithful ally of Syracuse, and also Athens; and he acquired considerable renown in the Greek world. He died in 367 and was succeeded by his son, also Dionysius, who inherited both his power and his aims and commitments in the Italian and Adriatic sphere (being encouraged in the latter by the admiral and historian Philistus, a former counsellor of the older Dionysius who had been exiled and was now recalled to Syracuse). However, his rule as tyrant was undermined by opposing political forces. Plato was involved in the ensuing conflict. Open civil war broke out when Dionysius was challenged by his uncle, Dion, at first an exponent of liberal and anti-tyrannical ideals and then, briefly, a tyrant himself. It is notable that a very important part was played by mercenaries. Even under the first Dionysius they made up the kernel of the army, and they had become the prop and symbol of tyranny. Some of them were Gauls, but for the most part they were presumably recruited among the Oscan-speaking Italic peoples – Samnites, Campanians, Lucanians – as was the chieftain Mamercus who succeeded, amidst the prevailing anarchy, in placing himself at the head of his compatriots and carving out a territory of his own at Catania.

As central power in Syracuse collapsed, the city's dominance came to an end and southern Italy was caught up in ever greater confusion. The pressure from the Lucanians reached its greatest intensity when the league of the Bruttians, in the heart of modern Calabria, was established (356). Deprived of their lands, the old Greek colonies struggled to hang on to their independence; some, such as Terina and Hipponion, were completely overwhelmed. In the years that followed, a fresh threat arose when the Messapians of Apulia embarked on a sudden surge of expansion. With the assistance of the Lucanians, they conquered Metapontum and Heraclea outright. This, evidently, meant the demise of Archytas' league. At this time the inhabitants of Apulia were themselves hard pressed and in part subjugated by the Lucanians.

Further north, too, these middle decades of the fourth century were particularly turbulent. Occasional references in the historical sources inform us that the Gauls continued to raid Latium and as far south as Campania, without any stable balance being established. Disbanded mercenaries pillaged the coasts of Latium. Volscians, Aequi and Latins came successively and variously into conflict with Rome, whose expansionist strategy, following the fall of Veii, had started to alarm the cities of southern Etruria, of which Tarquinii had assumed clear leadership. Among their other claims, the Tarquinians put themselves forward as exemplars and guarantors of an oligarchic form of republicanism. From 358 to 351, they made war on Rome, led by their general and chief magistrate Aulus Spurinna (whose eulogistic biographical epitaph has come down to us in a Latin inscription of the Roman imperial era). Aulus Spurinna defeated the monarchical regime of Caere, friendly to Rome since its burning by the Gauls, and crossed Caeritan territory to approach Rome by way of the mouth of the Tiber. However, this tactic did not succeed, and the war ended without practical results, except perhaps for a strengthening of the links between Caere and Rome. Tyrrhenian Etruria as a whole, and the more northerly cities in particular, seem to have remained fairly calm and prosperous during this period (though there were civil disturbances, a slave revolt, and later on factional struggles at Arezzo). But beyond the Apennines, the Etruscan phase was finally coming to its end. The Gauls had now taken possession of Bologna and Marzabotto, and the port of Spina was silted up and abandoned. Various sources mention 'Tyrrhenian pirates' as having been active in the Adriatic and even the Aegean during the fourth and third centuries. This may represent a resurgence of sea-borne enterprise on the part of remaining Etruscan groups, aided by the collapse of Syracusan control of the Po delta and perhaps also by a change in the attitude of the Gauls towards the now subjugated Etruscans.

A new page in the history of the Greek presence in Italy was turned when, almost at the same moment (343–342), the Corinthian Timoleon came to Syracuse and Archidamus king of Sparta came to Tarentum. From now on, political and military leaders intervened from the mother country with the aim of ending disorder and outside threats. Italy, as a result, became for some while a land of adventure and conquest. Timoleon moved shrewdly and cautiously, and his intervention proved beneficent and restorative. Greek Sicily, after the fissiparous excesses of government by tyrants and internal struggles, achieved a new unity. Individual cities retained their autonomy while acknowledging the leadership of Syracuse, where a moderately democratic regime now governed. We know little about Archidamus's expedition, but he presumably attempted to stem the influx of the Lucanians and Messapians: he met his death fighting the latter in 338. Some time later (the chronology is rather uncertain), the Tarentines invited in his place Alexander of Molossia, king of

Epirus and uncle of Alexander the Great. His campaigns were to have greater impact. He first set out to meet the most immediate threat to Tarentum, fighting and defeating the Messapians – with the assistance of other more northerly Apulian peoples, the Peucetians and the Daunians – and recapturing Heraclea and Metapontum. He also attacked the Bruttians and Lucanians, carrying the offensive right into the latter's territory to 'liberate' the former Greek colonies of the Tyrrhenian shore as far as Campania. Here, however, he came up against the Samnites, against whom he agreed a treaty of friendship with Rome. Back in the south, he routed the league of the Bruttians and took their capital, Cosenza.

Had death not put a sudden stop to his activities, Alexander of Molossia might well have restored Magna Graecia to its former glory, reversing or checking the conquests made by the Italic peoples over the previous decades. He appears to have envisaged the formation of a new Italiote league, centred on Thurii. Thurii's location was more suitable than Tarentum's – though at this time, and indeed throughout the century, Tarentum undoubtedly held first place, intellectually and artistically as well as politically and strategically, among the communities of Greek Italy. The Molossian's true intention, however, was to carve out a territory of his own in Italy, as Alexander the Great was doing on a much larger scale in his eastern conquests. This was another attempt at the imposition of hegemony from outside, following Dionysius of Syracuse and already in some respects anticipating the example of the Hellenistic kingdoms. Alexander the Great may have welcomed and given support to his uncle's enterprise, for several hints in the historical sources suggest that he harboured dreams of expansion in the west too. For instance, the Romans are said to have sent an embassy to the great Macedonian at about the same time as Alexander the Molossian was embarking on his expedition. Etruscans, Lucanians and Bruttians are mentioned among the western peoples represented at Babylon in order, presumably, to pay homage to Alexander. The largely unsuccessful campaign of Alexander of Molossia was followed by other outside interventions by the Greeks. Soon after, the Spartan prince Acrotatus attempted to defeat the Sicilian regime of Agathocles with the help of Tarentine ships (315–314). His brother, Cleonymus, who also hoped to establish a dominion of his own (which was why he seized Metapontum), embarked in support of Tarentum against the

Lucanians and the Romans. He then set out on a naval incursion into the Adriatic as far as the territory of the Veneti, basing himself at Corcyra (Corfu), whose fall marked the end of his adventures in the west (303–302). Finally, there was the great Italian expedition of Pyrrhus, king of Epirus, who found himself confronting the Romans, by this time (280–275) virtual masters of the Italian peninsula. This new strategic and political situation is described in the next chapter.

Events in the Mezzogiorno took a new turn during the final decades of the fourth century. The recurrent pattern of conflict between Lucanians, Bruttians, Messapians and Italiote cities was increasingly affected by the developing situation to the north. The Lucanians, the advance guard of Italic expansion, found themselves neighbours to a newly established and strengthened Samnite league. This powerful alliance controlled an extensive area in the heart of Italy between the Adriatic north of Daunia and Campania. On the Tyrrhenian, Rome was growing in political and military might since the Etruscans no longer posed a threat. Provoked by Rome's ambitions, the Latins of the old league centred on Aricia (and now dominated by Rome) united with the Volscians and the Campanians and sought war, in which they were defeated (340–338). This led to Roman domination of a large territory between southern Etruria and Campania. The Samnites and the Romans, initially oscillating between amity and enmity, eventually became firm foes. The bitter armed struggle between them lasted more than twenty years (326–304), and became a battle for supremacy in central southern Italy. Of broader historical import for the Italic world as a whole was the fact that Rome for the first time ventured outside its own geographical sphere, forging an early link with the Daunians of northern Apulia, who found themselves threatened by the Lucanians and probably also the Samnites. This irruption of Roman power into the southern Adriatic further complicated an already complex situation, and alarmed the Tarentines. But Tarentum forbade the Roman navies passage across the Gulf, thus vindicating – at any rate in theory – its claim to be the leading city of the former Italiote league of Archytas.

The end of the century saw a significant resurgence of Sicilian expansionism under Agathocles, a bold adventurer and unscrupulous tyrant who revived some of the strategic and political aspirations which had animated Dionysius at the beginning of the century. He had fought in Italy, and freed Croton from the Bruttians (330). As an ardent advocate of democracy, he was a suspect figure to the oligarchic regimes of the Italiote cities. In 318, he took power in Syracuse, and in 311 embarked on a long and bloody war against the Carthaginians, even leading his troops to Africa. But Carthage's Sicilian dominions remained largely intact. It is noteworthy that Agathocles was helped in this war by eighteen Etruscan ships, reversing Etruria's former pro-Carthaginian and anti-Syracusan policy. Here too, unless (as is quite possible) this was a merely casual initiative by some particular Etruscan city, we may see a reflection of the new situation created by the growth of Rome's power. Just at this time, the Romans were engaged in their victorious struggle with the Etruscan league (311–308), and they agreed a non-aggression pact with Carthage – themes to which we shall return. Having unified and pacified Greek Sicily, and having taken the title of 'king of the Siceliotes' (a gesture in imitation of the Hellenistic sovereigns), Agathocles set out to conquer southern Italy. He clashed several times with the Bruttians, and made an alliance with the Iapygians of Apulia. However, his supremacy seems not to have reached beyond modern Calabria or to have affected Tarentum's sphere of influence. Conversely, the conquest of Corfu, brief though it was, indicates his interest in the Adriatic and more generally in the Greek east. Agathocles' campaigns involved virtually all Italy, for his mercenary troops included Campanians and Samnites, Etruscans, Ligurians and Celts.

5

Roman Unification
and Italic Continuity

5

Roman Unification and Italic Continuity

Two parallel 'histories'

In 338 BC, Rome won its war with the Latin-Volscian-Campanian coalition, and this led to the creation of one of the peninsula's major political and regional structures. In 295, as we shall see, the battle of Sentinum ended in defeat for the grand alliance between Samnites, Gauls, Umbrians and certain of the Etruscans, and this allowed Rome to gain supremacy over the entire peninsula. This brief period, little more than a single generation, saw events which were to have decisive consequences for the whole history of the world of antiquity. A city-state (Rome) and a league (the Latin league), formally no different from the other city-states and leagues established in Italy by the Etruscans and Greeks, transformed themselves irreversibly, and almost miraculously, into a power that governed the fate of the Italic world and was capable of limitless further expansion. Hitherto, Romans and Latins had not been especially prominent in Italy as a whole. We may even say that Rome was politically and culturally less important than the Etruscan or Greek worlds. If Rome and Latium command our particular attention, that is because of what might be called a subjective factor – the fact that Rome, and by reflection Latium, are the focus of a historiographical tradition that allows us to explore even their earliest phases in a way impossible in other cases. Until the close of the fourth century, Rome and Latium are simply an aspect of the history of the Italic world in general.

However, the events outlined above marked an epoch-making shift. Rome became the leading actor on the Italian scene, and we may well claim that it was only from this time on that we can speak of a 'Roman history' of wide general significance. For all that, no neat line divides two historical eras, with 'Roman history' cancelling out and replacing 'Italic history'. We shall see throughout the present chapter that even in the new configuration, there was much continuity. Ethnic-linguistic structures and cultural and administrative forms persisted over much of the territory and among much of the population of the Italian area for at least two centuries, or in other words during what we call (following the chronological terminology of the Greeks) the Hellenistic period, from the end of the fourth until the beginning of the first century. Italic experience and consciousness coexisted with the admittedly and crucially new fact of Roman hegemony, and 'Italic history' continued to run parallel with 'Roman history'.

In their strategy and its implementation, the Romans used both armed force and considerable pragmatic and political skill to impose a single unified system. In this way, they superimposed a new pattern on the Italic tradition of pluralism with its many separate states, while preserving its forms intact – almost as if two realities coexisted on different levels. It is undeniable that Italy was substantially and radically transformed in this period. Where a multitude of forces had been in play, balancing one another or coming into collision, there was now a single unchallenged power. Where there had been incessant conflict, there was a peace guaranteed by the system of alliances with Rome. The entire territory of Italy was covered by a dense network of Roman and Latin colonies. Whereas in the past the world outside had impinged on Italy, Italy now took the active role, turning outward in the wars and conquests of the Romans. Economic and social conditions changed, too. Small and middling landed property declined and the *latifundia* and the institution of slave labour became widespread, while new capitalist classes arose alongside the old oligarchies.

For all this, there were strong and in some respects very obvious reasons for continuity. These can be approached from two points of view. First of all, Roman policy and strategy itself represented an epitome and a development of certain fundamental themes running through the Italian historical experience. We shall begin by considering this intrinsic continuity. In the second place, the most extensive territories and the most characteristic sectors of the Italic world (Etruscans, Umbrians, Samnites, Iapygians, Greeks) passed, often smoothly and almost inadvertently, from a state of complete independence to a condition of subjection to Rome within the framework of the great Roman-Italic federation. The passage was traumatic only in a few instances, and then only at the start. Here, there was armed conflict with Rome – the Samnite wars, the conflict with the southern Etruscan cities, the war with Tarentum. However, we can apply the term 'conquest' only in the case of those territories annexed or intensively settled by colonists, and these as a rule lay close to the dominant city itself, namely, Latium, Campania, a small part of Etruria, the Sabine lands and more generally Sabellian central Italy as far as Picenum. Elsewhere, alliance may have been compulsory and its terms onerous, but it did not abolish local autonomy, nor change the physiognomy of the local communities and their peoples' sense of ethnic identity. In other words, the Italic peoples must on the whole have regarded the imposition of Roman supremacy as an episode, not as the 'end' of their history.

As we shall see, that end came only when conditions within the Italic world itself and the demands of Roman expansion in the Mediterranean made it impossible to maintain the existing structure of the federal state and the status of its inhabitants. A legal simplification was required. This was achieved by annexing to Rome the entire territory of peninsular Italy through the granting of Roman citizenship to the relevant peoples. This was at the beginning of the first century BC, and was followed some decades later by the extension of this final process of Romanisation to embrace northern Italy as far as the Alps. After these events, it is no longer appropriate to speak of 'Italic history', but only of traditions that endured or revived: and these will be the subject of our epilogue.

The pacification of Italy

The wars waged by Rome in the closing decades of the fourth century and the opening decades of the third were at once the culmination of the struggles that had marked the battle-scarred fourth century and the basis on which peace within Italy was to be established. We shall endeavour to describe them from the various points of view from which they were experienced, through the eyes of both victors and vanquished. We shall outline a common Italic history, even if the present subject has particular relevance to the history of Rome.

We have already said that the Latins were decisively defeated in the war of 340–338. Their relationship with Rome had been fluctuating and ambiguous since archaic times: was Rome on a par with the other cities of the Latin league, or was it in fact supreme? Its real supremacy, which grew greater during the fourth century, provoked an armed response in 340. Rome pursued its own policy and its own interests in its dealings with the complex of communities with which it shared a similar origin, language and history, as was shown in its war with and conquests in Etruria. The Latins, for their part, had adopted a position distinct from and hostile to the Romans even in the archaic period, forming alliances with the Greeks of Cumae. They now sought support from the Volscians (old enemies of theirs, for they had conquered a large part of Latium), the Aurunci and the Campanians. This repeated turning to Campania foreshadows the trends of later Roman expansionism and the causes of the conflict between the Romans and the Samnites. Campania was a region of great geo-political importance, a meeting-place and battle-ground for the major ethnic protagonists of Italic history. Their defeat in 338 meant the end of the Latins' identity as a nation. Even their most immediate home territory was systematically broken up by the Romans, by a variety of measures – annexations, alliances, colonisations. The notion of *latinitas* and of Rome and Latium as two distinct entities was to survive only in the distinction made between colonies under Roman law and colonies under Latin law, corresponding to those founded by the Romans directly and by the Latin league. The difference was a matter solely of civic rights and laws.

One area of Tyrrhenian Italy had now been brought into subjection and pacified – if only for the time being. This new political entity, comprising the lands of the Latins, Volscians, Aurunci and some of the Campanians, bordered on the following lands and peoples: free Etruria to the north-west, the Italic peoples of the central peninsular region (Sabines, Aequi, Marsians, Peligni and others) to the north-east, and the Samnite league to the south-east. These peoples and groups must have regarded this upsurge in the activity of Rome as an untoward phenomenon, outside their traditional political horizons – which explains why generally they failed at first to perceive the danger that it posed. Over a brief period of time (before the close of the fourth century), Rome imposed on them, by force of arms and by diplomacy, a series of accords and sometimes of bilateral alliances. The resulting relationship oscillated ambiguously between the effective supremacy of Rome and the freedom of the federated communities to decide things for themselves. A hegemonic system that covered much of the peninsula, and which was about to extend its reach into northern Apulia, was taking shape.

However, this process took place by a variety of means. The Samnites, the most compact group, were engaged in outright war. The struggle was lengthy, slackening and growing more intense by turns. Fortunes fluctuated, but the superiority of Rome became ever clearer. The historical sources suggest that there had been earlier phases of hostility and friendship. In 326 conflict broke out once more, beginning in Campania, where the interests of the two powers clashed and where Rome was gradually enlarging its dominion in the aftermath of the Latin war. The Romans, with great strategic boldness, at once carried the battle to the frontiers of the Samnites' Apulian territory. They were warmly received by the local population, made up of Daunians and probably also of Peucetians, who had long been threatened by the Lucanians and Samnites and were keen to see the pressure lifted through the help of an outside force. An attempt was made to encircle the Samnite bloc, whose static and defensive tactics were in contrast to the Romans' aggressive energy. But the Romans suffered a setback when they were defeated in the Caudine Forks (321): the Samnites won control of Lucera, in Apulia, and of the colony of Fregellae in Volscian territory, while in Campania the cities of Nocera and Capua defected. However, the balance of advantage soon swung back towards Rome. In Apulia, the Latin colony of Lucera was founded (or refounded?) in 315. In Volscian lands, the route into Latium was blocked off. The conquest of Campania was resumed and completed. In the following years the war dragged on more or less wearily on two fronts (Adriatic and Tyrrhenian) until the Samnites made peace by concluding a pact of alliance (304). The new territory brought into the federation naturally embraced not only Samnium but the loyal Daunian area, including the major cities of Arpi and Canosa.

There are many connections between the course of the Samnite wars and the vicissitudes of the Roman subjugation of the eastern Italic peoples who lived to the north of Samnium. Roman action in Apulia necessitated accords with the Marsians, Peligni, Marrucini and Frentani (the latter, while of Samnite stock, seem not to have been members of the league), for Roman troops had no alternative but to cross their lands. They appear to have felt little mistrust or hostility towards the Romans at first: and the same is true of the Aequi and of those Sabines not as yet directly under the dominion of Rome. There was armed conflict with the Vestini, on the other hand. During the great struggle between the Romans and the Samnites, there were occasional defections on the part of these peoples, impelled perhaps by their sense of kinship with the Samnites. It is worth noting that in 310 the Samnites planned to send reinforcements into Etruria across Marsian and Sabine territory. However, the route into Apulia remained constantly open. In the end, all these peoples concluded peace treaties at the same time as the Samnites, entering into alliance with Rome, whose sphere of influence was thus extended to the central Adriatic region.

Only in 312 did disturbances break out in the third neighbouring zone, Etruria. Until this time, Etruria had remained completely independent throughout its vast area, except for Veii, which had been annexed, Caere, which was linked to Rome (the truce between them had been in force for many years and there was mutual citizenship *sine suffragio*, or in other words of an originally honorary and formal kind, conferring no electoral rights), and Tarquinii, with which a forty-year peace treaty was in force. At some point, determined no doubt by the progress of the Samnite war, the Etruscans, clearly perceiving the formidable extent of Roman power, must have decided and prepared to confront it. The historical sources speak of a collective campaign on the part of the Etruscan league, Arezzo apart, but one imagines that the major cities of north Etruria will in general have committed themselves less decisively to the war than did the cities of the south, above all Tarquinii and Volsinii. The combined Etruscan force strove in vain to seize the fortress of Sutri, which blocked the way into Roman territory. A Roman diversionary action, striking at the heart of Etruria, soon led the major northern cities of Perugia, Cortona and Arezzo to conclude a truce. In 308, the war came to an end following a series of setbacks suffered by the Volsinians and perhaps also by the Tarquinians,who had renewed their former forty-year truce. It is notable that the Romans did not at once conclude treaties of alliance with the Etruscan cities, even if this was what they sought: rather, the formula used was that of *indutiae* or truces. These may have implied greater recognition of the full independence in foreign policy of the nations with which they were concluded, but they were more provisional and in a sense more threatening. However, alliances were soon established, presumably one by one, though their dates cannot in every case be ascertained.

The growing power gained by Rome as a result of its expansion on land was matched by increasing activity at sea. Eventually, Rome supplanted the former naval powers of Caere to the north and Antium (Anzio) to the south, even though these cities had supported Roman interests (and here the 'naval allies' of Campania's ports come into the picture too). Two facts are especially interesting from the point of view of Italic history. In 306 BC, Rome and Carthage agreed a treaty which redefined their respective spheres of influence and thus amounted to a *de facto* recognition of Rome's supremacy over the Italian peninsula. Another accord, this time between Rome and Tarentum, probably in operation before the end of the fourth century, prohibited the Romans from sailing north of Cape Lacinium, or in other words the Croton headland. The agreement, barring them from the Gulf of Taranto, implicitly acknowledged the Romans' full freedom of naval action in the Tyrrhenian and southern Ionian.

Italy, however, was still far from being subjugated and pacified. The incredible speed with which Rome rose to military and political prominence during the last decades of the fourth century inevitably provoked a reaction throughout the Italic world. The Samnites and the Etruscans, keen for revenge, were joined by the Gauls, re-entering the fray and always eager to push down into the peninsula from their northern and Adriatic lands. The Umbrians, too, now became a factor in the course of history. In the late fourth and early third centuries, the war spread along various fronts. In Etruria, there was a whole series of truce violations and military actions. The Romans came to the assistance of the Lucanians against the Samnites, attaining their long-held objective of encircling Samnium (the eulogy on the tomb of Lucius Cornelius Scipio Barbatus claims proudly that the whole of Lucania was subjugated). This opened the possibility of contact by land with the Greeks – and aroused the hostile suspicions of Tarentum. At length, in 296, the coalition of the *quattuor gentes* or four nations was drawn up against Rome. This included not only the Samnites, but the Etruscans, the Gauls and the Umbrians: a fleeting glimpse of an Italy united independently of Rome, such as never had existed and never would exist. The Samnites under their chief Gellius Egnatius took the initiative, but the main concentration of troops was in northern Umbria, not far from the territory of the Gauls. The Gallic people in question must have been the Senones, a formidable and battle-hardened contingent. Gauls and Samnites fought virtually unaided in the great battle of Sentinum (Sasso-ferrato in the modern Marches), but their defeat meant the collapse of the coalition as a whole (295). At around the same time, the people of Clusium and Perugia were defeated in Etruria, and in the following year the same fate befell the Volsinians. Roselle was captured, and Volsinii, Perugia and Arezzo all signed fresh truces with Rome. For the time being, the Gauls had been put out of the picture. In the following years military operations continued in the central Apennine area, with the subjugation of the Sabines and the Praetutii, and around the Samnites' territory. Eventually the Samnites were obliged to make peace, following the disastrous defeat suffered by their chief Gavius Pontius and the foundation of the Latin colony of Venosa in the borderlands between Apulia and Lucania (291). New alliances were agreed, but the land was divided up and parts of it were annexed through the formula of citizenship *sine suffragio*.

Not many years later (from 285), fresh hostilities broke out in various parts of Italy. The Gallic tribe of the Senones advanced into Etruria, laid siege to Arezzo, and with the help of other Etruscans inflicted a bloody defeat on the Roman army which came to relieve the city. However, the Romans responded by invading the Gauls' home territory, the *ager gallicus* along the Adriatic coast, where they founded the colony of Sena Gallica (Senigallia). Meanwhile the Boii, another Gallic tribe, perhaps alongside the Senones and undoubtedly assisted by some Etruscans, made a bold raid aimed directly at Rome. This campaign foundered at Lake Vadimo, not far from Bomarzo in the middle reaches of the Tiber valley, where the raiders were heavily defeated (283). Meanwhile, fresh fighting had broken out in the south against the Samnites, Lucanians and Bruttians. Rome had taken the side of the Greek cities against which these Italic peoples had recently launched an offensive. Roman forces lifted the Lucanian siege of Thurii, establishing a garrison there (282). Locri and Reggio were subsequently sub-jugated. Thus Roman supremacy was accepted, peacefully and voluntarily, within the Hellenic world too. Tarentum remained the single exception. Its old dreams of being a great power had already encouraged it to oppose the Romans several decades earlier by blocking their advance into Apulia and setting limits to their naval expansion.

Tarentum, then, was the setting for the final act in the drama of Rome's pacification of peninsular Italy. When a number of Roman ships, perhaps without deliberate hostile intent, broke the naval blockade and appeared off the port, the Tarentines attacked and war broke out. This brought about the intervention of one of the most colourful figures of the Hellenistic world, Pyrrhus, king of Epirus, who came to the aid of Tarentum but soon assumed the leading role himself. Like his predecessors Alexander the Molossian and Cleonymus, Pyrrhus came to Italy with a powerful army, intent on carving out a large territory for himself (280). The Romans, already in conflict with Volsinii and Vulci in Etruria, now faced a new danger. They were twice defeated, at Heraclea and at Ausculum in Apulia (the terror caused by Pyrrhus' elephants is well known). The Lucanians and the Samnites staged a fresh uprising. Pyrrhus, however, proved unable to open up a route into central Italy, and chose rather to turn towards Sicily with the aim of conquering it and freeing it from the dominion of Carthage, which had formed an alliance with Rome (278). The venture failed, and Pyrrhus turned once more towards Rome, which had meanwhile restored order in the peninsula. He was defeated at Beneventum (275) and forced to return to Epirus. Tarentum then surrendered, submitting to the terms of an alliance with the Romans (272).

The subjugation of the peninsula had by now been effectively, and irreversibly, completed. In Etruria, there was spasmodic and belated anti-Roman agitation at Caere (274 or 273), and a Roman expedition was sent against Volsinii in order to restore the aristocratic ruling class dispossessed by a popular revolt. The city's location was moved from Orvieto to Bolsena in consequence (265). Etruria presented no further problems. The Samnites and Lucanians suffered further reductions of their territory and were obliged to accept terms of permanent alliance, concluded with separate groups as there was no longer any Samnite league (some limited defections from the Roman camp were to take place in this area during the second Punic war, through pressure brought to bear by Hannibal following the battle of Cannae, between 215 and 210). The third major ethnic area, that of the Greeks in Italy, was entirely absorbed into the federal state, from Tarentum through to Reggio, which was liberated in 269 from an occupation by Campanian mercenaries. Sicily, however, had hitherto remained outside the sphere of Rome's interests. It was still divided between the Carthaginians in the west and the Greeks in the east, the latter in a state of constant unrest and disunity since the death of Agathocles. Agathocles' Campanian mercenaries had taken possession of Messina, where they had founded the state of the Mamertini, called after their war-god Mamers or Mamars (Mars). When the Mamertini asked for help against the Carthaginians, the Romans were led to intervene in Sicilian affairs and this precipitated the outbreak of the first Punic war (264).

Northern Italy remains outside the picture we have been drawing. Although it had formed some earlier political and cultural ties with the peninsula (in particular, through the spread and influence of the Etruscans), it was in reality segregated from the rest of the Italian world, basically because it was so heavily occupied by the Celts. Only after the Roman conquest was it included in the denomination of Italy. This conquest came about under conditions very different from those in which Rome had subjugated the peninsular territories. By this time, the Romans were becoming a Mediterranean power. Between the first and second Punic wars, Rome defeated a hostile alliance of various Celtic peoples (at Telamon in southern Etruria, in 225). The Romans then invaded the plains of the Po, occupied the lands of the Boii, Lingones and Insubrians and founded the colonies of Cremona, Piacenza and Modena. However, these conquests were swept away when Hannibal entered Italy, and had to be laboriously re-established in the early second century. It is worth noting that the Veneti – unlike most of the Gallic peoples, who resolutely maintained their traditional hostility – adopted a pro-Roman stance from the outset, being absorbed uneventfully into the dominion of Rome.

The Tyrrhenian, eastern Italic and Greek heritage in Roman policy

I observed at the beginning of the chapter that Italic identity was not annihilated by the assertion of Roman hegemony over the peninsula. This was first of all because Rome's politics and actions were in some respects lineally descended from earlier Italic history. This is an internal rather than an external factor, inherent in the very development of Roman history. From this point of view, Rome reflects the most 'advanced aspects' of the history of the Italic world.

Let us first consider the 'Tyrrhenian' heritage, taking the term (here as before) to embrace all those cultures which flourished on the Tyrrhenian flank of the peninsula. These civilisations – the Etruscans, and to a lesser extent the peoples of Latium and Campania up to the point where it merged into the Greek colonial zone – had enjoyed their original and greatest flowering during the archaic period. Subsequently, their fortunes waned somewhat because of economic crisis and the invasions of the eastern Italic peoples and Celts. The historical focus shifted towards inland, northern and Adriatic Italy. It is possible to regard the rise of Rome and of its Romano-Latin-Campanian system, expanding from this geographical nucleus to dominate the peninsula, as nothing less than a renaissance of Tyrrhenian Italy, a kind of revenge against the Oscan-Umbrian-speaking races. Nor should this revival be thought a mere matter of chance, for a conscious and unbroken historical link joins sixth-century Rome, which had shared in the flourishing Tyrrhenian civilisation of archaic times, to the Rome of the fourth century, which ushered in a new political and strategic dispensation. As the Latin element triumphed in the history of Italy (and of the entire western world!), so traditions rooted in the life of the oldest historical communities of central western Italy developed and flourished on an unexpectedly vast scale.

Let us now consider the second aspect of continuity. The eastern Italic peoples had conceived and attempted an unprecedented project: territorial conquest of a type which, being capable of unlimited expansion, tended more or less consciously towards the unification of the Italian peninsula. (This is quite different from the earlier example of the Etruscans, whose expansionism confined itself to limited colonial areas.) This dynamic impulse underlay the success of the Oscan-Umbrian-speaking Italic people in penetrating into Latium, Campania, the Tyrrhenian littoral, part of the Apulian region, and Emilia. It also accounts for the constant harrying of the Greek cities of the Mezzogiorno as they pressed towards the sea on every side. They might have realised their goal had not the unexpected advent of the Romans altered the course of history. The eastern Italic peoples, of all the inhabitants of pre-Roman Italy, offer the clearest image (in the fourth century) of a 'national' grouping, centred in the very heart of the peninsula. Their leagues – Samnites, Lucanians, Bruttians – were mutually linked and as a rule jointly supportive. The Samnite league was the most important and cohesive. As we shall see, these ethnic groups already identified themselves with 'Italy' in antiquity, which is why today we often refer to them as peculiarly 'Italic'.

If we bear this in mind, we can hardly deny that the Romans, although they fought and defeated the Sabines, took over the historical role of the eastern Italic groupings. In a sense, they carried it to its completion. They pressed forward in an unstoppable territorial expansion until they reached the furthest limits of the peninsula, they took the place of the Lucanians in resisting invasion from abroad (when Pyrrhus landed), they created a unified political bloc – Italy – embracing the whole peninsula, and in time they extended both its frontiers and its name as far as the Alps. Moreover, between the third and the second centuries the Oscan-Umbrian-speaking element formed a very significant part both of the population of the Romano-Italic federation and of the auxiliary detachments of the Roman armies (making an important, if not indeed decisive, contribution to their Mediterranean conquests).

Once Italy as an entity had come into being, it immediately and inevitably confronted the problem of its relations with neighbouring Carthage. Since archaic times, Carthage had been an important accessory in the history of the Italian world. Arguably, it should not be seen as an altogether 'external' element: it ruled much of Sicily (as well as of Sardinia, where its dominion was less disputed), it had concluded alliances with Etruria (which may in some cases have amounted to a virtual Carthaginian protectorate), and it had intervened militarily in the struggles of southern Italy. Admittedly the Rome-Carthage treaty of 306, confirmed by the accords of 279, barred the Carthaginians from the peninsula.

Nevertheless, events in Italy were likely to be influenced by the presence of the formidable Carthaginian fleet in the waters of the Tyrrhenian and even the Ionian sea (the fleet was off Tarentum, for instance, when that city surrendered to the Romans). This was so particularly after the end of Agathocles' reign and the failure of Pyrrhus' campaigns, when the Greeks of Sicily were plunged into a most serious crisis which, had the Romans not intervened, might have proved terminal.

This intervention, which marked the outbreak of the first Punic war (264), takes on especial significance in the context of recent Sicilian events. The immediate reason why the Romans disembarked on the island was that they wished to assist the Mamertini against the Carthaginians, who had laid siege to one of their fortresses at Messina. Their decision no doubt also followed from the broader strategic imperative of safeguarding freedom of navigation in the Straits, or in other words retaining secure and unbroken control of the peninsular coastline. But 'mainland' solidarity with this portion of Italy lying beyond the water, and these Italians whose forebears had been enemies but who now fell under Rome's protection, was surely another factor. However, the Greeks of Sicily (like the Greeks of Magna Graecia before them) were now also attracting the attention of the Romans, who had established friendly relations with Hiero of Syracuse rather earlier, in 270. This move might be, and was, interpreted by the Carthaginians as violating the basic agreement about the division between Roman and Carthaginian spheres of influence. Both Italic and Greek peoples were thus involved in the outbreak of the conflict.

Let us now consider the problem in a wider perspective. Modern historians have seen that the Punic wars were in some respects a continuation of and epilogue to the centuries-old struggle between Carthage and the western Greeks. Here again there was surely an element of continuity between the pre-Roman world and the policy of Rome. Sicily and the seas around it had provided the military arena for the Deinomenids, Dionysius, Timoleon, Agathocles and Pyrrhus; they did the same for Duellius, Caecilius Metellus and Lutatius Catulus. When Agathocles had led his forces into Africa, they had met with the same unhappy fate as did those of Attilius Regulus: only the Scipios finally and decisively turned the tables, at the end of the second and third Punic wars.

The conquest of Sicily brought to an end ·the former division between the Greek and the Carthaginian worlds, which the balance of the two contending parties had never been able to resolve and which never would have been resolved had Rome not intervened. However, the defeat and destruction of Carthage belongs within a later and wider historical horizon. It exceeds the compass of the Italic world, and opens the way to Rome's Mediterranean and universal destiny. For that reason, it lies outside the limits of the present study.

Federated Italy: the Italic world between the third and first centuries BC

That the history of the peoples of pre-Roman Italy continues into the period of Roman dominance is plain from the fact that their ethno-linguistic, socio-political and cultural characteristics survived essentially intact – not just as inert, debilitated traditions, but with some capacity for further development. This avenue of approach has been more or less neglected by modern historiography with its stress on the leading military and political role of Rome. However, our claim is borne out by the fact that every one of the major surviving written testimonies concerning the religious and juridical culture of the Italic world dates from after the fourth century (in Etruria, we have the ritual manuscript of the Zagreb mummy and the Perugia cippus; in Umbria, the Iguvine Tables; and in the Oscan-speaking countries, the Agnone Table, the *Cippus Abellanus*, and the Bantine Table).

Politically, the peninsula took the form of what is usually known as the Roman-Italic federation. This was an aggregation rather than a system. A mosaic of different conditions and relationships, it was also an instrument of unitary power, a fluid and dynamic entity which, though provisional, was capable of further refinement. It had its defects, but it had the great virtue of conforming to reality. In summary, three types of bond were established between the Romans and the territorial units into which the peninsula had come to be subdivided, namely, annexation, colonisation and alliance. (There were also intermediate conditions, and in time a particular territory would often pass from one status to another.) In cases of annexation pure and simple, land was subsumed within

Figure 11 Italy in the third to second centuries BC.

Roman territory (the *ager Romanus*) and its inhabitants were granted Roman citizenship. There was a geographical logic to this process, which began in Latium and the Etruscan and Sabine areas closest to Rome, and continued towards Campania, along the Tyrrhenian coast of Etruria, and inland across the Sabine lands to the middle Adriatic shore. Within this process of incorporation, various gradual and special forms existed, such as *civitas sine suffragio* (in which the population enjoyed no electoral rights), the institution of 'prefectures', and the granting of citizenship under Latin law. Annexation by conquest might be the prelude to the forfeiture of colonies. These were constituted when contingents of Roman (in the case of Roman colonies) or Latin (in Latin colonies) citizens were transferred. These contingents were essentially and primarily military in nature, and the non-Roman lands to which they were sent might well be isolated and far from Rome. In this way, fresh outposts of Romanisation and Roman rule were created. Finally, we must consider the third type of link, which entailed no institutional dependence on Rome, namely the relation of alliance (*foedus*) which applied to most of the land and peoples of Italy. Here too – here, indeed, above all – we find a great variety of forms and provisions, explained by the variety of occasions, places and circumstances in which agreements were made. Sometimes, as with Camerino in Umbria or some of the Greek cities of the Mezzogiorno, the parties were formally regarded as equals (*foedus aequum* or *aequissimum*), but in most cases more or less onerous terms were imposed, especially as regards military assistance (*foedus iniquum*). In any event, political independence in theory and administrative, juridical and cultural autonomy in practice were assured to the allies (socii), and this was additionally termed *libertas* or *foederis libertas*.

It is logical that the way of life of the former Italic peoples should have persisted with the most marked continuity among those communities which became allies and in areas where annexation was less disruptive and colonisation brought least change. As we have seen, this applied to much of Etruria and Umbria; to various small historical 'islands' in Latium, such as Tivoli, Praeneste and Ardea; to the Sabellian peoples of the central Apennines such as the Marsians, Peligni and Marrucini; and to part of Campania, along with much of Samnium, Lucania, Bruttium, Apulia, and the former Greek colonial area. (Mention should also be made of areas outside the peninsula: certain zones of Sicily before the whole island was made into a Roman *provincia*, and, to the north, the communities of the Veneti in the second century. Northern Italy, at this time not yet formally part of 'Italy', is discussed below.) These were the major ethnic groups and cultural areas of Italic history: old Italy, and those who had played leading roles in it, were delivered over more or less entire to the experience of a new and final era.

This statement does however require some clarification and amplification. The extent to which the legacy of the Italic past was handed down depended on place and time. Ethnic and historical-cultural identity was most clearly preserved by those allies whose civilisation had been long-established, advanced and distinctive, who had entered relatively peacefully into Rome's orbit, or who had at any rate been insulated from the areas where wars of subjugation had been waged and colonisation had brought disruption and innovation. This was the case with the Etruscans, the Umbrians, and some of the eastern Italic peoples and inhabitants of Apulia (and also the Veneti). In Campania, local tradition remained very strong even where alliance was replaced by annexation with special status, as it was in Capua. In the extreme south, by contrast, the Greek cities were to suffer a progressive and irreversible decline, particularly in the aftermath of the second Punic war, and this led to their disappearance from the historical stage. Everywhere, moreover, old national characteristics and idiosyncrasies tended to fade as time passed. During the second century, the institutional terms of alliance remained substantially unaltered, but Romanisation became ever more pervasive. This was due above all to the increasing extent and use of the road network, to the fact that Roman and allied soldiers fought alongside one another in the army, and to the social and economic crisis discussed below, which affected all parties.

Relations between the various Italic peoples did not become any closer following the general submission to the power of Rome. This entailed a general pacification, and put an end to the old struggles for land and power which had stained the fourth century with blood. However, the Roman-Italic federation was not a mutual association of the Italic peoples: it was a matter of exclusively bilateral ties with Rome. There are nonetheless signs of some contact and exchange, particularly in religious and artistic ideas and practices. It is not always clear how far the evidence reflects a spontaneous convergence of different cultural spheres and how far it reveals the mediation and initiative of Rome: a little of both, perhaps, for Rome and Latium stood in the midst of a geographical area, stretching from Etruria down to the Italic and Greek Mezzogiorno, with a long history of civilised settlement and common development. Moreover, while the various peoples who made up the Roman-Italic federation may appear to have been isolated and immobile (for isolation and immobility were the outcome of the order imposed by Rome), there are signs that considerable population movements took place. The Samnites, for instance, appear to have moved towards Latium (at Fregellae) and into Apulia (at Lucera and Venosa), and this may even be interpreted as a continuation or resurgence of the large-scale ethnic migration of the eastern Italic peoples during the previous centuries, though its scope was more limited and it had acquired what might be called a 'private' character. Samnite influence at Fregellae was probably one cause of that Latin colony's revolt and subsequent destruction in 125 BC – the last defection from the Roman camp before the Social Wars. We also have records of population movements enforced by Rome, around the time of the wars of subjugation. The conquered Picenians were deported from the Adriatic to a stretch of Tyrrhenian land on the border between Campania and Lucania (the *ager Picentinus*) in 268. Forced resettlement of a purely local kind took place when the inhabitants of the allied cities of Volsinii and Falerii were moved, the former from what is now Orvieto to Bolsena (264) and the latter from Civita Castellana to Santa Maria di Fàlleri (241). Italic peoples were active outide Italy, acting on their own entrepreneurial initiative even if enjoying the favour and protection of Rome. We have evidence of this in connection with maritime trade in the eastern Mediterranean, one of whose principal centres was the free port on the Aegean island of Delos, and we know the name of one of the leading *negotiatores* of the second quarter of the second century, Trebius Loesius. Such merchants must have come above all from Campania. The presence of Italic emigrants, especially speakers of the Oscan language, has been inferred or hypothesised on the basis of place-name evidence not only in northern Italy but also in Mediterranean Gaul and the Iberian peninsula. What were the main characteristics of the civilisation and society of the Italic world during this phase of continuing vitality? Each people bears witness to its sense of national tradition by using its own language in written documents, which consist basically of inscriptions (indeed, entirely of inscriptions, except for the Etruscan fabric texts connected with the Zagreb mummy). But documents survive in notably greater quantity, and of notably greater interest, from this period than from earlier ages. So far as the Oscan and Umbrian languages are concerned, we can even say that the documentary evidence derives almost exclusively from the centuries of Roman hegemony. Latin began to take root and spread (the people of Cumae petitioned Rome in 180 for the right to employ it in public affairs: Livy, XL 42), but it did not supplant the traditional idioms until the general grant of Roman citizenship made at the beginning of the first century BC, which thus marked a fundamental break.

Written evidence, insofar as it has come down to us and even though it is very fragmentary, also reflects social structures, institutions and cults, and complementary evidence can be gleaned from archaeological remains in general. We also have the accounts in the historical sources – more valuable now than for preceding periods, because the historians are nearer in time to the period they are describing. Urban society was still found chiefly in Tyrrhenian and Greek Italy. However, colonial settlements that 'copied' the model of Rome or the Latin cities were spreading. The forms and institutions of city life were also borrowed and adopted by communities and population centres in the autonomous territories of the central Apennine, Adriatic and northern regions. This happened especially in Apulia and Umbria (where Gubbio, the Iguvium of the ancients, is a typical instance, on which much light is cast by the famous ritual texts of the Tables). Elsewhere, only a few tentative steps were taken in the direction of city life, and in such mountainous areas as Samnium and north-east Italy settlement remained centred, as in prehistoric times, around hilltop fortresses (known as *castellieri*, Latin *oppida*). The eastern Italic counterparts of the Etruscan and Campanian city-states were territories based on kinship – though it may have been mistaken to call such kinship-groups (Caraceni, Pentri, Caudini and Hirpini, in Samnium) 'tribes': the Oscan term, *touto*, more or less corresponds to the Latin *populus*. The Roman policy of divide and rule had put paid to the leagues of states so typical of the period between the fifth and the early third centuries, which had been found from

Etruria and Latium to Samnium, Lucania, Bruttium and the Greek cities. Only during the Social Wars, and then only briefly, was there a renewed grand alliance among the insurgent eastern Italic peoples.

The forms of government adopted in all these states were without exception decisively republican. There were elected magistrates and councils, and assemblies of various kinds, not unlike the Senate and *comitiae* of Rome. Most of the literary and epigraphic evidence about the qualifications and functions of the magistracy belongs to the period we are now discussing, but there is no doubt that the institutions originated before the Romans established their dominance (in the Etruscan case, this is proved by inscriptions dating back to the fourth and even the fifth century). A degree of uniformity seems to be implied by the existence in diverse contexts and linguistic forms of a title which signifies the right to exercise power in general. This is endowed with different attributes depending on the precise function involved – although the same title is also used, perhaps by antonomasia, to designate the supreme power. The term in Etruria is *zilc(h)* or *zilath*; in Campania and Samnium, *meddix* (*meddíss* in the original Oscan); in Rome, *praetor* (the term initially denoted the consuls); in Umbria, probably *maro (n)* (the same word in Etruscan, *maru, marunu-*, refers to another of the many political-administrative and religious offices recorded in inscriptions). The highest dignity was in general reserved for a single individual, and amounted to something like the presidency of the state (indeed in the Oscan area it was called, precisely, *meddix tuticus* or *meddíss tovtíks*). When we find two people exercising equal power, this is probably, though not necessarily, due to the influence of the Roman consuls.

The shape of these societies is reflected in their funerary and dedicatory inscriptions (the former are very abundant in Etruria, but scarce elsewhere). The use of two names, individual forename and family name, is typical of and restricted to the Italic sphere, with the exception of the Veneti and Messapians; it would appear to denote the status of freeman and the possession of civic rights or their equivalent. Slaves, whose status and position in the social hierarchy it is difficult to determine exactly, were excluded from the system of family lineage. In Etruria, they seem to have attempted on several occasions to gain freedom and power, most famously in the revolution at Volsinii in 265. In the cities of the north, however, especially Clusium and Perugia, elements of the slave population seem to have been absorbed relatively peacefully into the civic body during the second century, to judge by the number of personal names entering use as family titles. Within the system of family lineages, a small number of rich and powerful families predominated, both in Etruria where the old oligarchies had become more firmly established (leading families included the Cilnii at Arezzo, the Caecina at Volterra, and at Tarquinii – where inscriptions record them as having held public office – the Velcha, the Hulchnie who subsequently appear as the Fulginii, the Ceisinie or Caesennii, the Plecu, Partunu, Pinie, and others) and among the Campanian and Samnite communities (Egnatii, Gellii, Pontii, Papii, Magii). The dominant senatorial class at Rome gave its backing to these local aristocracies, seen as a stabilising factor. This system of local aristocracies might even be regarded as one of the chief reasons why the former nations of the Italic world were able to preserve their traditions and way of life.

We must note two points about the more visible characteristics of these civilisations – their religion, figurative art, architecture and town-planning, and technology. 1) Hellenistic influence was responsible for a large number of innovations, although it did not obliterate distinctively Italic qualities, which in some ways actually tended to enjoy an unexpected flowering. 2) This cultural pattern was particularly well-marked and pervasive, and shows signs of common development, within an extensive area corresponding roughly to the region covered by urban civilisation as it spread from the Tyrrhenian zone inland and towards the Adriatic region of the peninsula. Exotic beliefs and cults took root and flourished in new localities, as in the famous instance of the Bacchanalia. These mysteries, celebrating the god Dionysus or Bacchus, together with their associated sects and orgiastic feasts, flourished from southern Italy to Etruria, fomenting disorder and violence. In 186 BC the Roman senate took very severe measures, in which Rome's allies were obliged to participate, to suppress them. Various forms of divination also grew more common and widespread. Haruspic-ation, or the consulting of animal entrails, and the interpretation of thunderbolts and prodigies were all typical of Etruria, and augury or the interpretation of bird-flights was found both at Rome and among the Oscan-Umbrian-speaking eastern Italic peoples. Archi-tectural features unlike Hellenistic models and akin to local traditions can be seen in both temples and houses (houses with atria are found in particular at Pompeii during the so-called Samnite phase), and the same applies in artistic and craft production (where there was a preference for forms derived from geometry rather than nature, tending towards a violently heightened and expressionistic style). Today, we can identify an 'Italic' (or, as some would have it, 'middle Italic') artistic culture.

The major innovations that redrew the old map of Italy, and which were inevitably linked to the rise and development of Rome, occurred – especially in the second century – in the economic and consequently the social field. The spread of Roman supremacy had already stimulated and co-ordinated production (for instance, of Campanian black-varnished pottery ware, made in great quantity and found in a variety of places) and exchange. One mark of the Romans' practical efficiency was the fact that they took in hand the regulation of the monetary systems already in existence in Italy. (In the Greek cities of the Mezzogiorno, these were long-established and highly diverse, and many coins of artistic value were produced. In Etruria, minting of money was intermittent, and elsewhere it was scarcely practised.) Coins struck in Campania and Tarentum had to be stamped in Rome. The Roman mint began operating, adopting as its standard of weight the *as* – initially the libral or twelve-ounce *as* (327 gm), later the uncial *as* which weighed one-twelfth as much. Alongside these minted coins, cast coins (the *aes grave*) appeared and became widespread in the second century. They are found, as are numerous imitations of them, in the allied communities of Etruria and the central southern Italic area. Economic and social crisis in Italy, which followed Rome's major wars of conquest in Africa and the east, brought the large-scale capitalisation of wealth, a massive influx of slaves, the creation of *latifundia* (large estates), and the abandonment of their fields by free farmers, who converged on the cities and especially on Rome. This state of affairs must have harmed the weakest classes in the allied states, but there as at Rome it did no damage to the dominant aristocracy. It may have favoured the entrepreneurial classes equivalent to the Roman *equites* (though these did less well than their Roman counterparts from the profits made in conquests outside Italy). This may be why the allies showed little enthusiasm, and even some open discontent, when the Gracchi attempted to resolve the crisis by passing agrarian laws to confiscate and redistribute land. At all events, we shall shortly see that this crisis and its political repercussions set in train the process that led to the ending of Italic autonomy.

These remarks apply above all to the peoples of the peninsula, but they hold good in part for the northern territories within the Alpine crescent. These, as we have noted, were not as yet regarded as Italian. We must now say a few words specifically about them. Three major territorial and ethnic entities can be distinguished. To the west were the Ligurians, in part fused with the Gauls, but relatively unmixed in the mountainous Apennine regions of Liguria, Tuscany and Emilia, where they held tenacious and battle-hardened sway. To the east, the Veneti occupied a 'corner' of their own, while in the centre, spread over a very wide area, were the various Gallic peoples. We have already described Rome's wars in this area, and the vicissitudes of the Roman conquest of Cisalpine Gaul, which from the early decades of the second century onwards became subject to Rome. Here too we find the three forms – annexation, colonisation, alliance (the Cenomani, almost always loyal to Rome, were granted the status of allies). The Veneti were friendly allies. Both Veneti and Gauls kept their ethnic identity and something of their culture – but less perhaps, than did some of the major historical peoples of peninsular Italy, with their developed urban civilisation. The presence of many important Roman and Latin colonies as early as the first decades of the second century favoured Romanisation (Cremona, Piacenza and Modena were joined by Bologna and Parma, and by Aquileia in the Veneto). The Ligurians met a different fate. They were subjugated by force of arms and, later, by virtual police actions: the process lasted all through the second century. There is no clear development of local Ligurian culture visible before the beginnings of Romanisation (which commenced along the area's southern border with the foundation in 177 BC of the Roman colony of Luni).

The final clash between Italic consciousness and Rome: the Social War

After they came under the sway of Rome, the nations formed in the pre-Roman historical period retained not only their individual character but also their differences from one another. These were deep-rooted, resulting from the differing environments and experiences of the preceding centuries, and they naturally affected the various nations' relationship with Rome. If – to focus on the two major groupings in the peninsula – we compare the Etruscans with the Oscan-speaking peoples, it is clear that the latter were a younger force, more bellicose by tradition. They had less in common with the old, stable urban civilisations, and fewer cultural and geographical affinities with Latium, from which Rome had sprung. Their dealings with Rome may still have been a little coloured by memories of the bitter wars of the late fourth and early third centuries and of the partial revolt that occurred during Hannibal's invasions.

Against this background, we can assess the origins, course and historical significance of the striking event (or 'episode', though its consequences were not episodic) at the start of the first century. The Social War, called by Cicero the 'Italic war', at a stroke disrupted and reversed the process by which Rome and the Italic communities had seemed to be drawing closer and closer together.

This closeness had in fact been only partial. It had obtained much more in the cultural sphere than in politics or economics. It can even be said that during the second century and the earliest years of the first, a growing gap had opened up between the Romans (that is, citizens of Rome) and the Italic peoples (who lived in Italy but did not enjoy Roman citizenship). The Latins and those who were citizens with Latin rights occupied an intermediate position. When it came to important military, diplomatic and economic and financial decisions, Roman citizens certainly enjoyed a monopoly of power, leaving the Italic allies out in the cold. Italic peoples did take part in trade and other enterprises in the provinces created as Rome conquered territories outside Italy, but they were at a clear disadvantage compared with the active Roman entrepreneurs of the equestrian order. When the Gracchi brought in legislation to reform agrarian holdings, Italic possessions were included in the confiscations directed against those who had appropriated public land, but Italics did not on the whole benefit from the subsequent redistribution. Roman legionaries and contingents recruited from the Italic *socii* made the same sacrifices of effort and blood, but Roman generals were in command and economic and disciplinary treatment was very discriminatory.

Some acts bore the stamp of apartheid, for the number
and Italics allowed in Rome was limited, and the sons
marriages were debarred from Roman citizenship.

As Roman conquest spread, subjugating ever vaster areas, so
the condition of Italy grew more paradoxical and anachronistic.
Italy was a contributing factor in the power of Rome, and yet Rome
dominated Italy and excluded it from that power. As the citizens of
Rome came to enjoy ever greater privileges over the subject
peoples of the provinces into which the conquered lands were
divided, the Italic allies coveted citizenship all the more keenly,
even if they could obtain it only by forfeiting the political and
administrative guarantees they enjoyed – which now offered little
more than a façade of independence. This desire for Roman
citizenship – especially if the price was a general granting of such
citizenship – was not so keenly felt in more conservative areas such
as Etruria, and among certain social strata, namely the upper
classes. These people feared that innovation might affect their
economic advantages (especially in regard to land ownership) and
herald improvements in the condition of their subordinates.
Elsewhere – among the Italic peoples of central Italy, in Campania
and in Samnium – the clamour for parity with 'the Romans' grew
ever louder, and was echoed by political leaders. But the dominant
aristocracy of Rome was becoming increasingly determined to
reject whatever such moves were proposed by reforming
politicians (Gaius Gracchus and M. Livius Drusus).

By the late second and early first centuries, the Oscan-speaking
Italic peoples were impatient of their condition, recently made
worse by the growing burden of military conscription and by the
Gracchian reforms. When they were told that there was no
possibility of reaching a political settlement that would raise the
population of this large area of the peninsula from its second class
status, this was the final straw. Inevitably, if irrationally, they took
up arms, motivated by resentment rather than by any considered
judgement of what might be gained. They seized the chance which
arose when the Italic troops were partly demobilised during a
temporary lull in Rome's foreign wars. The enthusiasm and
ambition of various military and political leaders was another
decisive factor. These included Quintus Poppedius Silo and
Publius Vettius Scato among the Marsians; Gaius Vidacilius among
the Picenians; Gaius Pontidius and Titus Laphrenius among the

Vestini; Herius Asinius among the Marrucini; Marius Egnatius among the Frentani; Gaius Papius Mutilus, Numerius Lucilius, Numerius Statius, and Minius or Minatus Iegius among the Samnites; and the *meddix* Marcus Lamponius among the Lucanians. The spark that ignited the conflagration came when the tribune Drusus was murdered at Rome in the autumn of 91 BC. Drusus had been friendly with the Italics, who were said to have sworn a solemn oath of fealty to him. He was killed by an assassin in the pay of the oligarchic party. In reply, the agent Q. Servilius was killed, along with many other Roman citizens, at Ausculum (Ascoli) in Picenum. The revolt of the Picenians was accompanied by a more or less simultaneous uprising of the Marsians, the Peligni, the Vestini, the Marrucini, the Frentani, all the Samnites including the Hirpini, some of the Campanians, the Lucanians, and the northern Apulians (the fullest list is in Appian, I, 39 ff.).

The Social War did not involve the Etruscans (on whose dissimilarity from the eastern Italic world we commented above), nor the Umbrians (whose cultural and political ties by now tended to be with the Etruscan region), nor the Gauls and other northern peoples, nor, probably, the inhabitants of Apulia outside the direct influence of the Samnites or Lucanians, nor the surviving Greek zones. Widespread as it was, it seems to have been a phenomenon restricted to the Oscan-speaking Italic peoples; but it included all of these, from the central peninsular area down to the Mezzogiorno. We can thus detect a degree of 'national' unity, not previously manifested on such a scale. Yet even within this framework of provisional unity the inhabitants of the central area (Marsians, Picenians, Vestini, Peligni, Marrucini) differed from those of the south (Samnites, Campanians, Lucanians) in traditions, dialects and historical experience. It is in reference to all of Rome's enemies during the Social War that Roman antiquaries from Varro onwards begin to employ the term *Sabelli*. This properly applies to all those peoples who spoke Oscan, then, and not just to the inhabitants of the central area, as often in modern historians' usage: while the name *Sabini* or Sabines (of which Sabelli is a diminutive) should refer solely to the inhabitants of Sabina. This again follows the practice of antiquity and reflects the fact that the Sabines, who already enjoyed Roman citizenship, took no part in the revolt of their central Italian neighbours (and forebears).

However, the fact that the rising had a clear ethnic and linguistic identity and boundary need not prevent us from seeing a wider significance in this assertion of Italic claims vis à vis Rome. The insurgents took possession of the name 'Italy', whose actual meaning had been different (it had corresponded to Magna Graecia) but which now acquired a considerably wider geographical application, covering the entire peninsula. This seems to suggest a secret bond linking the deeds of the Sabelli to the destiny of all those who inherited the historical tradition of Italy as it had existed before the dominance of Rome – as if the needs and aspirations of that tradition were now being made manifest. The notion of Italy standing in opposition to Rome certainly seems to have become an ideological rallying-cry. Despite their parochial traditions and lack of urban development, the rebels made Corfinio in the territory of the Peligni the capital for their concerted resistance. The city, seen as Rome's counterpart, was renamed *Italia*. Money was coined bearing the image of the Italian bull crushing the Roman wolf (and the inscription *Vítelliú*, for 'Italy', referred back to the old derivation of *Italia* from *vituli*, Italian *vitelli*, 'calves'). Other coins showed an enthroned goddess (Italy?) being crowned by Victory: these reflected not only the hopes of those who minted them, but also probably the early course of the war, favourable to the Italians. Various coins were also struck by the different leaders and communites, to meet the needs of the moment but also as a sign of independence.

We can say, then, that a consciousness of Italian identity was now felt – strikingly, but belatedly and almost nostalgically – and proclaimed in opposition to Rome. It may well be asked how such a consciousness of opposition squares with the initial reason for the conflict, the demand made for Roman citizenship. Clearly, however, we are here dealing with a confluence of political motives and emotional impulses, which together brought about this paradoxical war – not so inexplicably, when we remember that the paradoxical situation of the allies was the cause of the conflict. Paradox, indeed, marked the whole course of the war.

The central Italic peoples, principally the Marsians, took the initiative and bore the brunt of the early fighting. This was why the conflict was at first known as the *bellum Marsicum*, and only later as the Italic or Social War. The great southern flank of the insurgent forces then assumed the burden of a more protracted struggle, though the entire war was extremely brief in terms of our overall chronology. The whole Sabellic front at once organised as a close-knit confederation (which perhaps suggests some advance preparation), different from the old Samnite league and its counterparts and rather resembling some of the leagues of the Greek world. There was a single five hundred member senate, probably made up of representatives of the various ethnic groups, and a political and military executive over which two supreme magistrates presided. Bearing the title of *embratur (imperator)*, these represented the two major divisions, the central Italic and the Samnian (Poppedius Silo and Papius Mutilus respectively were elected), and each was aided by six praetors. Rome was quick to do battle, deploying all its legions (not at this time active elsewhere) and swelling their numbers with an intensive recruitment drive. There was use too of Latin and provincial auxiliaries, and some Italic contingents who either remained unaffected by the revolt or had chosen to dissociate themselves from it. Minatus Magius led one such detachment, made up of bands of Hirpini. However, the warlike prowess of the Italics, fighting on their own united territory, proved too much, at least to begin with, for the surprised Romans. This explains the rebel successes of the year 90 BC: fighting was confused and geographically dispersed, stretching from the Adriatic coast to the territory of the Marsians on the central front and from Campania to Apulia in the south, but some significant events stand out, such as the defeat and death of the consul P. Rutilius Lupus, near Carsoli, and the conquest of Isernia (Aesernia) and Nola, which became fortified strong-points of the insurgents. The rebels, and especially their leaders in the central Italic sector, must now have aimed to open up the way rapidly for a direct thrust towards Rome. In this, however, they were unsuccessful, partly because the Roman commander in the field was the experienced Gaius Marius.

It was surely inevitable that the balance should eventually come down on the side of Rome, an organised power of long standing which enjoyed full control of more than half of Italy and dominated the seas and a great part of the Mediterranean littoral. In 88 BC, despite losing his fellow-consul L. Porcius Cato in the Fucino region, Gn. Pompeius Strabo succeeded in routing the Marsians and other central peoples, bringing his campaign to a triumphant conclusion by taking Ascoli, birthplace of the rebellion. In the south, meanwhile, L. Cornelius Sulla, exercising pro-consular powers, was sweeping through Campania (apart from Nola) and invading Samnium. The Italics moved their capital from Corfinio to Boviano, and from there to Isernia. The two Marsian heroes fell in battle: first Vettius Scato, and then Poppedius Silo, who had taken overall command of all the Italic forces. The recapture of Venosa, a former Latin colony which had fallen to the rebels at the outset of hostilities, was particularly important. No practical results attended the contacts made between the Italic peoples and Mithridates, king of Pontus, who had invaded the province of Asia and provoked the Romans to war. An expedition towards Sicily mounted by the Lucanians in Bruttium likewise came to nothing. In 87, civil unrest at Rome led to a lessening of the pressure on the Italic forces, reduced by this time to those in the southern sector, worn down by successive reverses but still holding the strong points of Nola and Isernia. An agreement was thus reached – and honoured – granting full citizenship to all those communities still in arms against Rome and allowing them to retain their war booty and have their prisoners back. Thus the conflict which had begun four years earlier in such a burst of anti-Roman fury fizzled out for the moment – without great trauma, and on terms quite favourable to the Italics.

The fact is that the old project of conferring automatic and general rights of citizenship on the Italian peoples had been accomplished through force of circumstances. As early as the first year of the war, the Romans feared that other allied communities, especially the Etruscans and Umbrians, might throw in their lot with the rebels. The *lex Iulia de civitate Latinis et sociis danda* was proposed by the consul L. Julius Caesar in 90 BC, and approved the same year. It offered civil rights to all those Latins and Italics who as yet lacked them, on condition that they were not in arms against Rome or else were prepared to lay them down forthwith. It was given further and fuller form in the *lex Calpurnia de civitate sociorum* and the *lex Plautia Papiria*. During the same period the whole of northern Italy received Latin citizenship in the *lex Pompeia de Transpadanis*. Presumably the inhabitants of the Cispadine region, corresponding to Emilia, had already been admitted to citizenship or were somehow given the same status as the Italic peoples of the peninsula. This legislation, rapidly passed and more or less rapidly implemented, satisfied those of the allies who had not been involved in the fighting – the Etruscans, Umbrians, Gauls and so on. Undoubtedly it also undermined the unity and resolution of the rebels, and must be accounted one of the causes of the gradual decline in their fortunes. However, it did not eliminate all the more emotional and 'nationalistic' sentiment that had spurred them to war; moreover, it did not even offer adequate guarantees of citizenship fully equivalent to that enjoyed by Roman citizens. It aimed to enrol the new citizens of the central southern Italic region in one of a small number of tribes, thus reducing the power and effectiveness of their votes in the *comitiae* (this indicates the persistence of opposition in the Senate to any meeting of the Italic peoples' wishes). When the tribune Q. Sulpicius Rufus attempted to remove this discrimination, it cost him his life thanks to the violent reaction of Sulla. He met the same fate as Gaius Gracchus and Livius Drusus. However, Marius's democratic party resumed the initiative while Sulla was away from Rome, engaged in the war at Pontus. In 87 BC, efforts were successful. This led to a reconciliation between Rome and the Italic peoples.

At this point, the issues of the Social War merge into those of the Civil War. Sulla returned from the east in 83, and although his return was accompanied by a general assurance that the rights which the Italic peoples had been guaranteed, and had acquired, would be respected, an extremely bitter attack was in fact launched against the new citizens (or those about to become such). Mostly these felt a natural loyalty to the Marian political party, which had favoured them. The Etruscans, friendly towards Marius and his followers, now took a leading role once more, joining in the fight against Sulla and his generals. They were heavily defeated at Clusium (Chiusi). Volterra was taken by storm at the end of a long siege, and forced – like Populonia – to accept very harsh terms. Sulla's forces established military colonies not just at Volterra but at Clusium, Arezzo and Fiesole. Meanwhile Samnite forces commanded by Pontius Telesinus and one of his brothers had made common cause with the anti-Sullan resistance. This alliance was bloodily and decisively defeated in battles at Sacriporto (Colleferro), before the gates of Rome (Porta Collina), and finally in its last redoubt, Palestrina (82 BC). Sulla's hatred of the Samnites continued to find expression in a series of harsh punitive expeditions into the mountains of Samnium.

Thus the history of Italy's pre-Roman peoples sank gradually during the first decades of the first century BC into melancholy decline. These events were the death-throes of nationalist and particularist feeling and culture. But they also opened up the prospect of convergence, in which each race would make its own fruitful contribution. Antithesis would be reconciled in synthesis. As a date, 90 BC is in a sense no more than symbolic. In fact, Romanisation was implemented slowly (there were even temporary reversals, as when Sulla deprived the inhabitants of Volterra and Arezzo of their citizenship). Sulla's repression was accompanied by other disruptive and ruinous events. Spartacus and his horde of rebel slaves laid a trail of destruction across southern Italy (72–71), Catiline's Etruscan followers were defeated at Pistoia (62), and most importantly Perugia was conquered, sacked and burned by Octavian, and its elders massacred. This 'Perugian war' of 41–40 is recorded by Propertius (*Elegia*, II, 1, 29) as the destruction of the Etruscan nation. All this, along with the requisitions and colonisations of Caesar and Augustus, helped to weaken and dissolve the strands of social, cultural and linguistic tradition still surviving in the communities of the peninsular Italic world. In northern Italy, events took a different course. Here, the influence of Roman models had been broadly and rapidly pervasive – all the more so, perhaps, because the area lacked its own forms of advanced civilisation – but only at the end of the Caesarian age was the right to Roman citizenship widely and generally extended to its inhabitants, in the *lex Roscia de civitate Transpadanorum* of 49 BC. There were probably other provisions too. The process culminated in the abolition of the province of Cisalpine Gaul by the Triumvirs in 42. Under Augustus, the whole of Italy, from the Straits of Messina to the Alps, was finally placed on the same footing.

Epilogue: survivals and revivals

The passage of the Italy of antiquity from plurality to unity – in laws and institutions, in language, in culture – marks the end of a historical cycle, and of our own journey in time. But this is to sum up or simplify a complex reality, and it is only in terms of a rough overall chronology that we can date the change to the beginning of the first century BC. Nonetheless there *was* a radical transformation, in that centuries-old national communities, linguistic traditions, religious conceptions and political entities, which had

had a more or less unbroken existence, now disappeared totally and irreversibly, their place taken by the new structures imposed by Rome. Whether and how far this resulted from the dominant power's overwhelming and destructive impact, as opposed to the will of the subject peoples, or whether it was the ineluctable consequence of time and circumstances, has long been a matter for controversy, some of it rather simple-minded. In any case, the question lies outside the scope of an objective historical account.

However, the fact that the peoples of pre-Roman Italy no longer enjoyed independent vitality does not mean that they became altogether extinct. The inhabitants of Roman Italy were, after all, the descendants of the inhabitants of pre-Roman Italy (setting aside the marked increase in immigration which also occurred, from the eastern Mediterranean and from other regions of the Empire) – and this applies to the Romans and Latins themselves. Ways of life changed, but the demographic stock remained. Families continued to descend from father to son, as is evident in the lexicon of personal names, where patrician appelations clearly betray, for all their Latin guise, their varied ethnic origins (Etruscan, Oscan, Venetic, Gallic or whatever). The general imposition of Latin, and the disappearance of other languages, is the most conspicuous mark of the passage from the old to the new historical dispensation, but we must not forget that Latin is not an extraneous element, but part of the linguistic heritage of the old Italic world.

In reality, Roman civilisation in late Republican and early Imperial times was to a large extent built up from bricks provided from various parts of Italy, though obviously we find the common form of the unitary Roman socio-political system, of Hellenistic-Roman ideas and mores, and of the Latin language. This is particularly clear in the field of literature. From the beginning of the third century on, the most famous Latin poets and writers include authors who were not Roman by birth. There are Italic figures of the most varied descent. Livius Andronicus was from Tarentum, Naevius from Campania; Plautus was an Umbrian from Sarsina, Ennius (with his 'three hearts', Greek, Oscan and Latin) was from Rudiae in the Salento region, Cato the Censor came from Tusculum, and Varro was a Sabine from Rieti. Cicero was from Arpino, Catullus from Verona, Sallust from Amiterno, Virgil from Mantua. Horace was an Apulian from Venosa, Propertius an

Umbrian from Assisi, Ovid was from the Peligni of Sulmona, Livy was of Venetic stock from Padua, and Velleius Patercolus was a Campanian descended from the family of the Magii. Statius was another Campanian, from Naples; Persius was an Etruscan; Pliny was from Como. Later, we find Italic people figuring, though (as is understandable) less prominently, in Roman political and social life. Members of various Etruscan families gained access to the Senate, the Consulate and other positions of high authority. In the second century, these already included the Perperna, Numisii and Aburii (these cases resulted from the former granting of Roman citizenship to particular individuals). There then followed, amongst others, the Caesennii, Tarquitii and Volcacii, as well as the Caecina, Aconii and Rufii from Volsinii, who remain prominent until late Imperial times. L. Elius Sejanus, famous as a minister under Tiberius, was also from Volsinii. M. Salvius Otho, whose family originated from Ferento, came to wear the Imperial purple, as later did C. Vibius Trebonianus Gallus from Perugia, in the third century. Maecenas, of course, enjoyed great influence in Augustan Rome. Counsellor to Augustus, Maecenas was a subtle and refined intellectual proud of his descent from the Cilnii of Arezzo. Another figure of the Caesarian and Augustan period was the politician and man of letters C. Asinius Pollo, nephew of Asinius Herius, the chieftain of the Marrucini during the Social Wars. During late Republican and early Imperial times we quite frequently encounter other personalities from the Oscan-speaking Italic world, some of whom bear distinguished family names such as the Poppaedii, Magii and Pontii: Pontius Pilate, Prefect of Judea, may be among the latter. The Flavi, who reached supreme power, were a Sabine family from Rieti.

However, these admittedly interesting instances are really no more than visible signs of the natural general continuity of the Italic peoples within the new blend of Roman Italy. Interestingly, Italic elements predominated in the early phase of unification, whereas later, beginning as early as the first century AD and more and more clearly in later Imperial times, people from the provinces came to play a complementary and eventually predominant role in politics and literature. In this sense, and bearing in mind also what was happening in the economy, religion, the composition of the army legions, and so on, it can be said that there was an early stage in which Roman identity was prevalently Italic, followed by a stage in which it was universal (as formally ratified in the granting of Roman citizenship to all the subjects of the Empire by Caracalla in 212 AD).

The history of the Italic peoples bequeathed to Roman life and civilisation a legacy not just of personalities, but of patterns of settlement and association. Virtually every Roman city was of pre-Roman origin. (The exceptions include colonial foundations such as Alba Fucens, Aquileia, Augusta Taurinorum which is modern Turin, Augusta Praetoria which is Aosta, and so on. There are also centres whose names express hopes and wishes, such as Placentia which is Piacenza and Florentia which is Florence, though here there are sometimes signs of earlier habitation. Finally, there are the *fora* or markets like Forum Iulium, which gives its name to Friuli, and Forum Livium, which is Forlì.) The pre-Roman names – Greek and Latin, Etruscan, Umbrian and Oscan, Apulian, Venetic and Celtic; and very often having more distant, pre-Indo-European origins – all persist under their Latin guises. A great many have persisted in Italian form down to the present day. Everywhere, over the centuries, life went on, even if its forms changed and the urban landscape slowly altered – although the Etruscan walls at Perugia remained in use as ramparts until the Renaissance, while the centre of Naples still bears traces of the plan of the Greek town. There is good evidence that certain ethnic groups persisted at a local level into the Roman Imperial age, especially in northern Italy and above all in the Alpine region. In any case it can be assumed that aspects of local or regional tradition connected with former national identities must almost everywhere have resisted the tremendous impact of Romanisation during the first century BC. Such traditions must have been handed down in one way or another to later times. This applies in the case of cults rooted in particular sites, which take on attributes of Greco-Roman religious practice and may even be transferred to Christian uses, as with those female deities that merge in the image of the Madonna. We find the same thing with folkloric survivals of very ancient customs and superstitions, especially in southern Italy. In language and linguistics, the vocabulary of Latin was enriched by words borrowed from various earlier Italian idioms (and modern Italian in consequence includes terms such as *persona, popolo, milite* which are of Etruscan origin). This apart, it seems that certain peculiarities of Italian dialects may derive from the influence of the pre-Latin substratum, especially in matters of phonetics. There may be echoes of Oscan in the Mezzogiorno and of Gallic in the north. It is more doubtful, though not impossible, that the aspirated speech of Tuscany derives from Etruscan. In such southern centres as Naples, Greek continued to be spoken throughout antiquity. The isolated Greek-speaking areas of Calabria and Apulia are generally regarded as attributable to the period of Byzantine domination, but it has been convincingly argued that we should trace their roots back at least in part to the world of the old Greek colonies.

Territorial names survived as a kind of fossilised memorial of the old peoples. We pointed out at the beginning of the present essay that when Augustus divided Italy up, the resulting regions bore the clearest possible relation to earlier ethnic-historical units. This was not a piece of antiquarianism; it was a lasting reality of human geography, though it also reflected a desire for orderly systematisation. Nine of the eleven regions have historic names. The first includes both Latium and Campania, perhaps in deference to the fact that these two had been linked by a special bond since the fourth century BC. The second designates Apulia in general – the central and northern parts of modern Puglia province, together with the Salentine peninsula (Roman Calabria with its Salentine population) and a westward extension taking in the territory of the eastern Italic people known as the Hirpini. The third corresponds to modern Basilicata and Calabria, the first known as Lucania, the second being associated with the Bruttians (it is notable that no mention whatever is made of the Greeks). The fourth groups Samnium together with part of the territory of the central Sabellic peoples (Sabines). The fifth, Picenum, runs along the Adriatic littoral between the rivers Aterno and Esino; as well as the lands of the Picenians of old, it includes those of the Praetutii and, in part, the Vestini. The sixth indicates that the term Umbria now included the Adriatic area of the old *ager Gallicus* (incorporated into Rome's dominions, as we have seen, as early as the third century). The seventh covers the historical territory of Etruria, with a limited extension taking in the Ligurian lands of Luni. The ninth incorporates the old Ligurian region up to its conventional boundary at the Po, while the tenth brings together Venetia and Histria. Only the eighth and eleventh regions lack ethnic-historical names. The eighth, Aemilia, took its name from the Via Aemilia which ran through it, but was also known as Gallia Cispadana. The eleventh, the Transpadana, is a geographical usage ('the lands beyond the Po', corresponding in modern terms to northern Piedmont and Lombardy) which should in any case be understood to stand for Gallia Transpadana. Northern Italy as a whole continued to be called Gallia for a long time – *Gallia togata* (the *togata* being equivalent to 'Roman'). The former extra-Italian provinces of Sicily, Sardinia and Corsica were brought into the classificatory scheme late in antiquity, but otherwise it remained largely as Augustus had drawn it up, though there were minor modifications (for instance, Sabina was detached from Samnium and took the name Valeria after the road that ran through it, and Umbria became part of Etruria, now known by preference as Tuscia). Echoes of the old scheme can still be heard in the Middle Ages, despite innovations stemming chiefly from ethnic and political factors. (Lombardy arrives on the scene, called after the Longobardi; Romagna emerges in eastern Emilia; in eastern Umbria and northern Picenum, Pentapoli appears, later known as the March of Ancona; Lucania changes to Basilicata; the name Calabria comes to denote the modern Calabrian region instead of the Salentine peninsula). They are still heard at the dawn of modern times, when the learning of the humanists helped revive the records of the traditional names and lands. The regional subdivisions of modern Italy are in many ways modelled on the old pattern, even retaining most of the names, slightly modified in some cases: Liguria, Venezia and the Veneto, Emilia, Toscana, Umbria, Lazio, Campania, Puglia, Calabria, Sicilia, Sardegna.

The Italic world bequeathed to Roman civilisation a rich cultural inheritance. In particular, many Romano-Latin traditions passed directly into the life of late Republican and Imperial Rome. There must certainly also have been a variety of other institutions, customs and public displays. These included some aspects (and perhaps the basic conception) of the municipal organisation prevalent in Roman Italy, where a city whose inhabitants were Roman citizens and which formed part of the Roman state enjoyed a measure of administrative autonomy, with self-government by a local magistracy, and possessed its own lands (the *municipium*). In the religious domain, the divinatory practice of haruspication was of Etruscan origin, as also, probably, were the customary funeral rites, in which the dead were borne along in procession, accom-

Figure 12 The regions of Italy unified under Rome in the Augustan period.

panied by musicians and by portraits of their ancestors. The heritage of ceremony and custom included the public display of the Triumph; the young horsemen's games, the *lusus Troiae*, known in Etruria from the seventh century BC; and gladiatorial games, originating in Campania, and perhaps passed on by the Etruscans. In literature, the Atellan theatre, with its farcical parodies, derived from Atella in Campania. In the arts, the official mainstream with its Hellenistic or classicising tastes was paralleled by popular or local production of painting and sculpture, and here we find further development of the abrupt, geometric and expressionistic forms typical of the Italic world during its final phase of independent cultural life.

There seems no doubt that very clear appeals were sometimes made to Rome's Italic roots in the course of Imperial history. Sometimes these related to general ideological, political and social themes, sometimes they reflected the antiquarian leanings of particular individuals and circles (not that we can always make the distinction). In the concluding stages of the unification of Italy and of the transition from republican government to the principate, Octavian took as his slogan the defence of Italic tradition against the oriental ways of Antony (and of his own adoptive father, Caesar). This is how we should see the Augustan restoration – a 'return' to ancestral virtues and also, it was hoped, a renaissance of peace and prosperity. In practical terms, old institutions and cults were revived: ideologically, Augustus' policy at once reflected and inspired the literary circle that surrounded him. Its patron, Maecenas, was an Etruscan and its highest expression, in the poetry of Virgil, celebrated warlike Italy and all its ancient peoples in the *Aeneid*, and pastoral and agricultural Italy in the *Georgics*. Among Augustus' noteworthy initiatives was the reconstruction of Veii: the city of antiquity became Municipium Augustum Veiens. This singular act of homage to the past of a famous adversary of Rome was as romantic, perhaps, as Propertius' recent lines with their image of Veii laid waste and annihilated (*Elegia*, IV, 10, 27–30).

Since the learned lexicographer and Etruscan scholar Verrius Flaccus was made tutor of the emperor's nephews Gaius and Lucius Caesar, the study of ancient Italy was presumably favoured and cultivated in the Augustan court. This was the environment which helped form the character of the learned Tiberius Claudius

Drusus, the future Emperor Claudius: the interest they both took in memorials of the past forms a link between Augustus and Claudius. Claudius, like Verrius Flaccus, wrote about Etruscan antiquities, and we have evidence of his historical learning in a discourse given to the Senate in 48 AD. His speech, concerning relations between ancient Rome and the Etruscan world, is reported in an inscription on a bronze tablet at Lyons (*Corpus Inscriptionum Latinarum*, XIII, 1668). He lent his authority to a pedantic and short-lived proposal to reform the Latin alphabet by introducing various innovations, among them a reversed letter *F*, reminiscent of the Etruscan digamma, to represent consonantal *u* or *v*. He must have been in contact with descendants of the Etruscan aristocracy, presumably through the influence of his wife Urgulanilla, who may have come from Caere. He also maintained links with the cities of Etruria. Caere dedicated a statue to him, and also – apparently – a monument. A fragment of this has survived, a piece of relief-work showing the symbolic images of three of the cities of the old Etruscan league.

We do not know what became of this league following the fall of Volsinii during the first half of the third century. Some of its sacred or ludic customs may even have survived the passage of the years. What we do know for certain is that it was renewed in the age of imperial Rome, though whether this official and scholarly revival was promoted by Claudius or by Augustus before him remains in doubt. At all events, we have concrete evidence of it in inscriptions, dating from the first century through to the fourth, that refer to the titles of *praetor Etruriae* or *praetor (Etruriae) quindecim populorum* (clearly the twelve Etruscan confederates had become fifteen) and of *aedilis Etruriae*. These were conferred on Romans of various ranks. The first title was the highest. The Emperor Hadrian in fact held it, along with various local offices brought back to life in his honour – dictator of Latium, demarch of Neapolis, and (outside Italy) archon of Athens (Spartianus, *Vita Hadriani*, in *Historia Augusta*, 19, 1). There is no doubt about Hadrian's interest not only in Etruscan traditions (and this may be to do partly with the rise to prominence during his reign of several figures connected in one way or another with the Etruscan world) but in Italian traditions generally, as well of course as in those of Greece and the Orient. The old Etruscan league in its revived imperial form must obviously have been concerned essentially with religious ceremonies, spectacles, circus games and the like. Presumably the titles we have mentioned were not merely honorific, but reflected the organisation and presidency of these celebrations. Following the custom of the ancients, these apparently took place – or had been moved back – 'near Volsinii' (perhaps on the original site of the Fanum Voltumnae?). This is made clear in the famous rescript of the Emperor Constantine found at Spello in Umbria, which permitted the townspeople to celebrate the festival at home without undertaking the journey to Etruria. Here we see clearly the impact on local tradition of the Emperor Diocletian's recent administrative provision which united Umbria with Tuscia in a single region (it is possible that their joint ceremonies were presided over by a *coronatus Tusciae et Umbriae*, named in another inscription found at Spello that also dates from the fourth century AD).

The formal conventions of Italic art left their mark not only on work produced for popular use or in the less important and peripheral Italian centres, but also on the provinces of the Empire. Here we observe a factor of some sociological interest. These conventions along with other habits and customs, took root after being carried to the furthest frontiers of Rome's dominions, especially in Europe and Africa. They were transmitted by legionaries, and also (if to a lesser extent) by Roman administrators – men, at least during the first century of the Empire, of overwhelmingly Italic extraction. These simplifying and expressionistic styles, typical of Italic tradition, merged with local modes to produce the characteristic figurative art of such areas as Gaul and Germany. In Rome itself, meanwhile, there was a reaction against the dominant classicism of official art. This may have been furthered by the changed composition of the ruling class. The old social order based on the great Roman dynasties with their senators and their members of the equestrian order was thinning out or disappearing, as people flooded in from the provinces and as groups from lower strata gradually climbed in the social scale. Classical forms gave way to a cursive style, passed on in an underground tradition beneath the Hellenising surface. A major 'change of style' became evident during the second half of the second century AD. It can be seen both in large-scale works and in particular expressive details, for instance in the reliefs of the Column of Marcus Aurelius and in the imperial portraiture of the third century, which at times strikingly recalls Italic sculpture of some centuries earlier. Here, the series of transmissions and innovations begins which was to lead to the artistic modes of late antiquity and the middle ages.

In other respects, too, the late classical and medieval periods echo far-off motifs from Italy's pre-Roman civilisations. The *haruspex* or augur, sacred counsellor of military and political leaders, died hard, lingering along with the last pagan rites until the fourth and even the fifth century AD. During these later times, scholars collected and preserved all kinds of fragmentary evidence about the world that had vanished centuries ago, but which still kindled people's interest. We see this in the analytic notes and evocations of early Italy in commentaries on Virgil's *Aeneid*, especially the one compiled by the grammarian Servius. We see it in the lexicographical work of Hesychius and others, with its records of words from the forgotten ancient tongues, and in the discussions of religious doctrine, especially among the Etruscans, produced by Christian and Byzantine writers such as Arnobius and Johannes Laurentius Lydus.

It is clear, however, that memories and memorials of the Italic peoples were bound to remain submerged within the great flood of historical tradition handed down from antiquity through the middle ages to modern times. Absorbed and suffocated by the Greek and Latin literary heritage, they faded and were lost in our picture of the classical world. Only with the Renaissance did they slowly begin to acquire their own distinctive outline, which grew ever clearer in subsequent centuries, thanks above all to archaeological discoveries and the investigation of surviving monuments. Recent generations have pursued the trail with growing enthusiasm, and today we are still rediscovering and interpreting these peoples and assessing the contribution that they made to history.

Chronological Table

	Events in the Italian area	Principal events in the rest of the Mediterranean
16th–15th centuries BC	Middle Bronze Age (Appennine) civilisation – Peoples speaking various types of Indo-European language already present in Italy, with some intermixture between themselves and with the indigenous populations – Mycenaean influences (Mycenaean I and II)	Flowering in Greece of the late Helladic (Mycenaean) culture – Mycenaean conquest of Crete – in Egypt, rule of the Eighteenth Dynasty: Egypt dominant in the Near East
14th–13th centuries BC	Late Bronze Age (late Appenine or sub-Apennine) civilisation – Mycenaean influence at its height (Mycenaean IIIA and B), with probable presence of Mycenaean visitors in southern and Tyrrhenian coastal Italy and the islands	Mycenaean political-economic system: centralised power, wide presence in the Mediterranean – Nineteenth Dynasty in Egypt and flowering of the Hittite empire in Asia Minor – first movements of the Peoples of the Sea
c. 1200		traditional dating of the Trojan war
12th–11th centuries BC	Final Bronze Age ('Proto-Villanovan') civilisation – ethnic movements: Iapygians into Apulia; Ausonians, Sicels, etc. into Aeolian Is. and Sicily – last phase of Mycenaean influence (Mycenaean III C) and weakening of links with Aegean	Crisis in eastern Med. and Near East: 'Peoples of the Sea' (Plst, Trš, Šrdn, Šklš, etc.: possibly connected with Italian area) – decline and break-up of Mycenaean system – sub-Mycenaean and protogeometric styles of pottery
10th century BC	last stage of Late Bronze Age civilisation – regional differentiation begins, related to future ethnic groupings	possible start of Phoenician voyages and colonisations in the west

171

	Events in the Italian area	*Principal events in the rest of the Mediterranean*
9th century BC	Iron Age civilisation: different forms in different ethnic groups: 'Palaeo-Italic' in fossa-culture area, Iapygian in Apulia, first eastern Italic peoples in middle Adriatic and central Apennine area, Latins in Latium, Etruscans in area of Villanovan culture, palaeo-Veneti in Ateste cultural area – Villanovan expansion northwards (Emilia-Romagna) and southwards (Salerno region)	Oligarchic regimes replace Greek monarchies – formation of the *polis* – civilisation characterised by geometric style Phoenician cities in western Mediterranean
c. 800		foundation of Carthage
8th century BC	Etruscan voyages towards southern Tyrrhenian and start of Etruscan 'thalassocracy' – pottery in geometric style arrives in Tyrrhenian Italy	Greeks begin to undertake voyages and colonial expeditions to the west
c. 775	Greek colony of Pithecusae founded on Ischia by Euboeans, Cumae on Campanian coast founded shortly after	
c. 750	Euboeans found Naxos, Megarians found Megara Hyblaea in Sicily marked development of late Villanovan civilisation in Etruria – social differentiation, emergence of a ruling class – formation of cities in Etruria, Latium, Campania (753 is the traditional date of Rome's founding)	
c. 730	Corinthians found Syracuse	
c. 715–710	Achaeans found Sybaris and Croton, Laconians (Spartans) found Tarentum first orientalising influences in Tyrrhenian Italy – introduction of alphabetic (Euboean) script in Etruria	orientalising fashions spread in Greece

		Events in the Italian area	*Principal events in the rest of the Mediterranean*
7th century BC	c. 700–670	Rhodians and Cretans found Gela, Locrians found Locri Epizephyrii, Greeks from Colophon found Siris	
		orientalising civilisation reaches full development in Etruria, and affects Latium – Caere and Praeneste flourish – Sabines at Rome	
	c. 650	Selinus founded from Megara Hyblaea	rule of tyrants at Corinth: Kypselos (657–627), Periander (627–585) – marked flowering of Corinthian civilisation and power – 'Daedalic' and Peloponnesian art develops in Greece
		Corinthian influence – developed orientalising stage – terracotta begins to be used as decorative material for building	first eastern Greek long distance voyages in the west: Kolaios of Samos reaches Tartessus in Iberia
	c. 615	the Etruscans at Rome ('period of Tarquinius Priscus') – culmination of Etruscan 'thalassocracy' and trade, as well as of Etruscan expansion by land	maritime expansion of the Phocaeans – founding of Massalia (Marseilles)
	c. 600	possible first incursion of Celts into northern Italy	
			Solon's reforms at Athens
6th century BC	c. 580	Greeks from Cnidos and Rhodes in Aeolian Islands – Agrigento founded from Gela	social and civil conflict at Miletus
		Sybaris flourishes in southern Italy	
		Vulci flourishes in Etruria	
	c. 575–530	possible start of social and civil conflicts in central Italy – exploits of Mastarna and the	Carthage rises to prominence among the Phoenician cities in the west

	Events in the Italian area	*Principal events in the rest of the Mediterranean*
	Vibenna brothers – 'Servian period' and reforms attibuted to Servius Tullius	
545		Cyrus king of the Persians conquers Asia Minor – Phocaeans flee to the west, joining other Phocaeans already established in Corsica
c. 540	Etruscan-Carthaginian coalition against Phocaeans of Corsica – naval battle of the Sardinian Sea – in consequence, Etruscans establish control of Corsica, and Carthage takes first steps towards conquest of Sardinia	
535–530	Phocaeans fleeing Corsica found Velia – Samians found Dicaearchia (Pozzuoli) – Pythagoras in Italy	
	Eastern-Greek (Ionic) art spreads widely in Italy	
	possible alliance of Sardinians (Serdaioi?) with Sybaris against the Carthaginian threat	
c. 530–510	reaction and tyrannic rule at Rome: 'period of Tarquin the Proud' – Rome gains dominion over Latium	
525	Etruscans at war with Cumae: they are defeated and Aristodemus rises to prominence	
510–509	Sybaris defeated and destroyed by Croton	time of the ending of tyranny at Hippias and introduction of democracy in Athens
	traditional date of the fall of the monarchy and the founding of the republic at Rome — first treaty between Rome and Carthage	
	expansion of Clusium – king Lars Porsenna at Rome	

	Events in the Italian area	*Principal events in the rest of the Mediterranean*
c. 504	battle of Aricia: Aruns Porsenna is defeated by Aristodemus of Cumae allied with the Latins	
	Sardinia conquered by the Carthaginians: the campaigns of the Magonids	
5th century BC 499–498		Ionians revolt against the Persians in Asia Minor
495	Anaxilas tyrant at Reggio	
490	probable approximate period of the pro-Carthaginian tyranny of Thefarie Velianas at Caere – beginning of Volscian penetration into Latium	first Persian war: Darius' offensive, battle of Marathon – Massalian Greeks defeat Carthage at Cape Artemisium
485	Gelon tyrant at Syracuse	
480	victory of Gelon over Carthaginians at Himera	second Persian war: battles of Thermopylae and Salamis; followed by battles of Plataea and Mykale (479), which conclude the war
478	Hiero tyrant at Syracuse	
477		start of '50 years of peace' in Greece – dominance of Athens – naval league of Delos
474	naval battle of Cumae: Etruscans defeated by Hiero and the Cumaeans	
473	successful Messapian offensive against Tarentum: possible Messapian advance as far as Reggio	
	development of inland Etruscan cities and flourishing of Po-Adriatic region of Etruscan civilisation (Bologna: civilisation of Certosa, Marzabotto, Spina)	
468	Appius Herdonius the Sabine makes an incursion into Rome	

	Events in the Italian area	Principal events in the rest of the Mediterranean
460–451	campaigns of Ducetius, the Siculan chieftain	period of greatest flowering of Greek civilisation, literature and art – Athens under Pericles
454–453	expeditions of Syracusan admirals Phayllus and Apelles against the seas and northern coasts of Etruria	
	Athens, on the initiative of Pericles, attempts to establish a footing in southern Italy and Sicily	
446–444	pan-Hellenic foundation of Thurii on site of Sybaris	
c.440–430	Samnites press on Campania: formation of the Campanian people	
431–421		first phase of the Peloponnesian war between Athens and Sparta (Archidamian war)
423	Samnites occupy Capua: end of the Etruscan dominion in Campania	
420	Cumae occupied by the Campanians: moves towards Greco-Campanian condominium at Neapolis	
415–413	Athenian expedition against Syracuse – an Etruscan contingent (perhaps from Tarquinii, under Veltur Spurinna?) fights alongside the Athenians, with some military success – disastrous overall outcome of the campaign	
413–404		last phase of Peloponnesian war and final defeat of Athens by the Spartans and Persians
409	Carthaginian counter-attack in Sicily: capture of Selinus and Himera	

		Events in the Italian area	Principal events in the rest of the Mediterranean
	406–404	Carthaginians conquer Agrigento, Gela and Camarina – Dionysius takes power in Syracuse	
4th century BC	396	Romans take and destroy Veii	
	c. 390	Gallic incursions in central Italy and along the Adriatic coast – constitution of the Lucanian league	
	387–383	Dionysius consolidates his power and pursues expansionist policies – capture of Reggio – Adriatic campaigns – foundation of Ancona – entente with the Gauls	
			dominance of Sparta
	c. 386	Gauls set fire to Rome	
	384	Dionysius' fleet sacks the sanctuary at Pyrgi	
	383–374	war between Dionysius and Carthage in alliance with Italiote cities and Lucani – Archytas' Italiote league	
	371		Athenian revival – battle of Leuctra – Thebes dominant
	367	death of Dionysius, accession of Dionysius II and start of phase of anarchy in Syracuse and Sicily	
		probable period of Tarquinian dominance in Etruria	
	358–351	Tarquinians under ⸱ɪ Aulus Spurinna make war on Rome – king of Caere dethroned – operations in Latium – slave revolt at Arezzo	
	356	league of the Bruttii formed – Lucanians exert growing pressure on Italiote cities – threatening presence of	Philip of Macedon begins expansionist policy in Greece

	Events in the Italian area	Principal events in the rest of the Mediterranean
	Messapians who conquer Metapontum and Heraclea	
343–342	Timoleon at Syracuse – Archidamus king of Sparta at Tarentum	
340–338	Rome's victorious war against the Latins, Volscians and Campanians – formation of a Roman-Latin-Campanian league	
338		battle of Chaeronea and imposition of Macedonian dominion on Greece
336		death of Philip and accession of Alexander the Great
334–323		Alexander's conquests in the east, followed by his death
c. 333–330	campaigns of Alexander of Molossia in southern Italy	
326–304	Rome at war with the Samnites – Roman relations with Apulia	
318–289	Agathocles tyrant of Syracuse and thus king of the Siceliotes (Greeks of Sicily) – he makes war on Carthage, with Etruscan help, and mounts an expedition into Africa – his campaigns in southern Italy	
315–314	Acrotatus of Sparta's Sicilian expedition	
311–307	Etruscans at war with Rome	
306	Roman-Carthaginian treaty granting Italy to Rome, Sicily to Carthage	
303–302	Cleonymus of Sparta's southern Italian expedition: he makes an alliance with Tarentum against the Lucanians	

		Events in the Italian area	Principal events in the rest of the Mediterranean
3rd century BC	296–295	anti-Roman coalition of Samnites, Gauls, Etruscans and Umbrians – Samnites and Gauls defeated at Sentinum – Roman victories over the Etruscans	
			Hellenistic civilisation and art in Greece and under the Diadochi in the Orient
	c. 285	Agathocles' Campanian mercenaries found the state of the Mamertines at Messina	
	285–282	Roman victories over the Galli Senones – conquest of the *ager Gallicus* – battle of Lake Vadimo – hostilities against the Samnites, Lucanians and Bruttians – Roman occupation of the Greek cities of southern Italy (Thurii, Locri, Reggio)	
	280–272	Rome makes war on Tarentum – Pyrrhus king of Epirus in Italy: his initial victories over the Romans and unsuccessful expedition against the Carthaginians in Sicily; he is defeated at Benevento (275) and leaves Italy – Tarentum surrenders	
	265	popular revolution at Volsinii: the Romans conquer the city and move its site	
	264–241	first Punic war	
	224	Gallic coalition against Rome – battle of Telamon – in consequence Romans occupy Gallic lands in the Po plain	
	218–201	second Punic war – Hannibal in Italy	
2nd century BC	199–196		Rome's war with Macedonia – start of Roman campaigns and conquests in the eastern Mediterranean with the military aid of the Italic allies
		Rome reconquers northern Italy	

		Events in the Italian area	Principal events in the rest of the Mediterranean
	186	Repression of the Bacchanalia: the Dionysiac cult widespread amongst the Italic allies	
	166		free port at Delos – Italic *negotiatores* become active in the Orient
	149–146		third Punic war: destruction of Carthage – Rome's domination of the Mediterranean is definitively confirmed
		gradual admission of elements of the slave population to citizenship in northern Etruria	
	134–132	slave war in Sicily	
	133	agrarian reforms and death of Tiberius Gracchus	
		discontent among the Italic allies	
	125	revolt and destruction of Fregellae	
	123–121	laws proposed favouring the Italic allies; death of Gaius Gracchus	
1st century BC	91	killing of Livius Drusus the tribune, favourably disposed to the Italic peoples, and outbreak of the Social War involving Oscan-speaking peoples of central and southern Italy – proposal of the *lex Iulia* granting Roman citizenship to Italic peoples	
	90–87	continuation and gradual fading out of Social War – Marius and his democratic and pro-Italic party in the ascendant at Rome	Italians massacred in the Orient and war with Mithridates king of Pontus – possible contacts between Mithridates and the Italic insurgents
	83–82	Sulla returns from the east and carries out repressive policies towards Italic elements –	

Events in the Italian area	*Principal events in the rest of the Mediterranean*
Samnite contingents defeated at the battles of Sacriporto, Porta Collina and Palestrina – Sulla acts against the Etruscans	
72–71 Spartacus' slave war	
49–42 provisions for the granting of Roman citizenship to the northern Italian populations	
41–40 war with Perugia: end of traditional Etruscan milieu	
1st century AD 27 BC–14 AD rule of emperor Augustus	
41–54 AD rule of emperor Claudius	
117–138 AD rule of emperor Hadrian	
late 2nd–3rd century AD Italic traditions reassert themselves in official Roman art	
4th–5th centuries AD last evidence concerning the activities of the *haruspices* (augurers)	

Bibliography

A general list is first given, in alphabetical order of authors (or of titles in the case of collective works). It includes publications which deal with the problems of Italy's pre-Roman history or which illuminate those problems in terms of the perspective of the present study. The books and articles listed represent genuine critical and scholarly contributions: secondary works and popularisations are not included. The general list is followed by detailed references for each of the present work's chapters.

Adriani, M., *La tematica 'Roma–Italia' nel corso della storia antica*, in *Studi Romani*, XVI (1968), pp 134–148.

Alföldi, A., *Early Rome and the Latins*, Ann Arbor 1965.

Altheim, F., *Italien und Rom*, I, Amsterdam–Leipzig 1941.

Atti del V Congresso Internazionale di Studi sulla Sicilia antica, in *Kokalos*, XXVI-XXVII (1980–1981) (contains lectures and discussions on aspects of the history of Sicily and peninsular Italy).

Aufstieg und Niedergang der römischen Welt, I: Von den Anfängen Roms bis zum Ausgang der Republik, 4 vols, plus vol. of plates, Berlin–New York 1972–1973 (a collection of essays by various authors referring to the history and civilisation of pre-Roman Italy: these are the initial volumes of an extensive collection).

Beloch, K. J., *Römische Geschichte bis zum Beginn der Punischen Kriege*, Berlin–Leipzig 1925.

Bérard, J., *La colonisation grecque de l'Italie méridionale et de la Sicile dans l'antiquité*, Paris 1957 (2nd ed.).

Bernardini, E., 'Problemi della monetazione dei confederati italici durante la guerra sociale', in *Rivista Italiana di Numismatica*, LXVIII (1966), pp 61–90.

Bianchi Bandinelli, R. and Giuliano, A., *Etruschi e Italici prima del dominio di Roma*, Milan 1973.

Bibliografia topografica della colonizzazione greca in Italia e nelle isole tirreniche, under the editorship of G. Nenci and G. Vallet, I–VII, Pisa–Rome–Naples 1977–1989.

Braccesi, L., *Grecità adriatica*, Bologna 1977 (2nd ed.).

Il bronzo finale in Italia (Atti della XXI Riunione dell'Istituto Italiano di Preistoria e Protostoria, 1977), Florence 1979.

183

Brunt, P. A., 'Italian Aims at the Time of the Social War', in *Journal of Roman Studies*, LV (1965), pp 90–109.
— *Italian Manpower 225 BC–AD 14*, Oxford 1971.

Calderone, S., Ἡ ἀρχαῖα Ἰταλία, in *Messana*, IV (1955), pp. 77–124.
Casson, L., *Ancient Mariners. Seafarers and Sea Fighters of the Mediterranean in Ancient Time*, London 1959.
Ciaceri, E., *Storia della Magna Grecia*, 3 vols, Milan–Rome 1927–1932 (2nd ed.)
Cianfarani, V., Franchi Dall'Orto, L. and La Regina, A., *Culture adriatiche antiche di Abruzzo e Molise*, Rome 1978.
Civiltà del Lazio primitivo (exhibition catalogue, with introduction and papers by various authors), Rome 1976.
Colonna, G., see 'Scavi nel santuario etrusco di Pyrgi'. . .
— 'Ricerche sugli Etruschi e sugli Umbri a nord degli Appennini', in *Studi Etruschi*, XLII (1974), pp 3–24.
Couissin, P., 'Guerriers et gladiateurs samnites', in *Revue Archéologique*, XXXII (1930), pp 235–279.

De Francisci, P., *Primordia Civitatis*, Rome 1959.
Della Corte, F., 'Su un "elogium Tarquiniense"', in *Studi Etruschi*, XXIV (1955–56), pp 73–78.
De Sanctis, G., *Storia dei Romani*, 4 vols., Turin 1907–1923.
— *La guerra sociale*, Florence 1976.
Devoto, G., *Gli antichi Italici*, Florence 1967 (3rd ed.).
— *Scritti minori*, II, Florence 1967 (this brings together writings concerned with the problems of the Italic world, especially in the spheres of linguistics and cultural-historical studies: of especial historical interest are the sections entitled *Umbri ed Etruschi*, with articles of 1930, 1938, 1960, 1965; and also the sections *Protolatini*, article of 1942; *Leponzi*, article of 1962; *Le origini tripartite di Roma*, art. of 1953; and *Tarpea*, art. of 1958).
— 'Storia italica', in *Rivista di Filologia e d'Istruzione Classica*, XCVII (1969), pp 257–267.
Ducati, P., *L'Italia antica dalle prime civiltà alla morte di C. Giulio Cesare*, Milan 1938.
Duhn, F. von and F. Messerschmidt, *Italische Gräberkunde*, 2 vols, Heidelberg 1924–1939.
Dunbabin, J. J., *The Western Greeks*, Oxford 1948.

Felletti Maj, B. M., *La tradizione italica nell'arte romana*, Rome 1977.
Fogolari, G., 'I Galli nell'Alto Adriatico', in *Antichità Altoadriatiche*, XIX (1981), pp 15–42.
Franchi Dall'Orto, L., see Cianfarani, V.

Frankfort, T., 'Les classes serviles en Etrurie', in *Latomus*, XVIII (1959), pp 3–22.

Frederiksen, M., see *Italy before the Romans*. . .

Furumark, A., *Det aldsta Italien*, Uppsala 1947.

Gabba, E., 'Le origine della Guerra Sociale e la vita politica romana dopo l'89 a.C.', in Athenaeum, XXXII (1954), pp 41–114, 293–445 (and also in *Escercito e società nella tarda repubblica romana*, Florence 1973).

— 'Perusine War', in *Harvard Studies of Classical Philology*, LXXV (1971), pp 139–160.

— 'Il problema dell' "unita" dell'Italia romana', in *La cultura italica* (Atti del Convegno della Società Italiana di Glottologia, Pisa 1977), Pisa 1978, pp 11–27.

— see *La Sicilia antica*.

I Galli e l'Italia (exhibition catalogue, various authors), Rome 1978.

Gamurrini, G. F., *Bibliografia dell'Italia antica*, 2 vols., Rome 1933–36.

Garbini, G., see 'Scavi nel santuario etrusco di Pyrgi'. . .

Le genti non greche della Magna Grecia (Atti dell'undecesimo Convegno di Studi sulla Magna Grecia, Taranto 1971), Naples 1972.

Giannelli, G., *La Magna Grecia da Pitagora a Pirro*, Milan 1928.

— *Trattato di storia romana, I: L'Italia antica e la repubblica romana*, Rome 1953.

Giuliano, A., see Bianchi Bandinelli.

Göhler, J., *Rom und Italien*, Breslau 1939.

Harris, W. V., *Rome in Etruria and Umbria*, Oxford 1971.

Hatzfeld, J., *Les trafiquants italiens dans l'Orient hellénique*, Paris 1919.

Hellenismus in Mittelitalien (Göttingen colloquium of 1974), Göttingen 1976.

Hencken, H., *Tarquinia, Villanovans and Early Etruscans*, 2 vols, Cambridge (Mass.) 1968.

Herbig, R., 'Die italische Wurzel der römischen Bildniskunst', in *Das neue Bild der Antike*, II, 1942, pp 85–99.

Heurgon, J., *Trois études sur le 'ver sacrum'*, Brussels 1957.

— *La vie quotidienne chez les Etrusques*, Paris 1961; revised ed., 1979; Italian ed., *La vita quotidiana degli Etruschi*, Milan 1963.

— *Rome et la Méditerranée occidentale jusqu'aux guerres puniques*, Paris 1969; revised Italian ed., *Il Mediterraneo occidentale dalla preistoria a Roma arcaica*, Bari 1972.

Hofmann, A. von, *Das Land Italien und seine Geschichte*, Berlin–Stuttgart 1921.

Homo, L., *L'Italie primitive et les débuts de l'impérialisme romain*, Paris 1953 (2nd ed.).

Ilari, V., *Gli Italici nelle strutture militari romane*, Milan 1974.

'L'integrazione dell'Italia nello stato romano attraverso la poesia e la cultura proto-augustea', various authors, in *Università Cattolica, Contributo dell'Istituto di Storia Antica*, I, Milan, pp 146–175.

L'Italie préromaine et la Rome républicaine, Mélanges offerts à J. Heurgon, 2 vols., Rome 1976 (includes writings by various authors which are to various degrees relevant to the history of pre-Roman Italy).

Italy before the Romans. The Iron Age, Orientalizing and Etruscan Periods, edited by D. and F. R. Ridgway, London–New York–San Francisco 1979 (a collection of writings, some previously published, which all help to cast light in one way or another on the history of Italy's pre-Roman civilisations in their earliest phase. The contributions of greatest interest are: R. Peroni, 'From Bronze Age to Iron Age: Economic, Historical and Social Considerations'; J. de la Genière, 'The Iron Age in Southern Italy'; D. Ridgway, 'Early Rome and Latium: An Archaeological Introduction'; M. Pallottino, 'The Origins of Rome: A Survey of Recent Discoveries and Discussions' (see also M. Pallottino, *Saggi di antichità*); M. Frederiksen, 'The Etruscans in Campania'; and J. and L. Jehasse, 'The Etruscans and Corsica').

Jehasse, J. and L., see *Italy Before the Romans*.

Klinger, F., 'Italien. Name, Begriff und Idee im Altertum', in *Römische Geisteswelt*, Munich 1967 (4th ed.), pp 11–33.

Krahe, H., *Die Indogermanisierung Griechenlands und Italiens*, Heidelberg 1949.

Kruta, V., 'Les Boïens de Cispadane. Essai de paléoethnographie celtique', in *Études Celtiques*, XVII (1980), pp 7–32.

— 'Les Sénons de l'Adriatique d'après l'archéologie (prolégomènes)', in *Études Celtiques*, XVIII (1981), pp 7–38.

La Genière, J. de, see *Italy Before the Romans*.

Lambrechts, R., *Essai sur les magistratures des républiques étrusques*, Brussels–Rome 1959.

Le lamine di Pyrgi (Tavola rotonda, Rome 1968; Accademia Nazionale dei Lincei, Quaderno no. 147), Rome 1970.

Langlotz, E., *L'arte della Magna Grecia*, Rome 1968.

La Regina, A., see Cianfarani, V.

Lejeune, M., 'La romanisation des anthroponymes indigènes d'Italie', in *L'onomastique latine* (Colloque du CNRS, Paris 1975), 1977, pp 35–41.

— *Ateste à l'heure de la romanisation (Étude anthroponymique)*, Florence 1978.

Lepore, E., 'L'Italia nella formazione della communità romano-italica', in *Klearchos*, V (1963), pp 89–113.

Levi, M. A., *L'Italia antica, I: Dalla preistoria alla unificazione della penisola*, Milan 1968.

Liou, B., *Praetores Etruriae XV Populorum (Étude d'épigraphie)*, Brussels 1969.

Loicq, J., 'Les Celtes en Italie (1965–1975)', in *Études Celtiques*, XV (1978), pp 655–703.

Magna Grecia e mondo miceneo (exhibition catalogue), Taranto 1982.

La Magna Grecia e Roma in età arcaica (Atti dell'ottavo Convegno di Studi sulla Magna Grecia, Taranto 1968), Naples 1971.

Maiuri, A., *Saggi di varia antichità*, Venice 1954 (a collection of previously published articles, including 'Problemi di archeologia italica' (1946)).

— *Arte e civiltà dell'Italia antica*, Milan 1960.

Mansuelli, G. A., 'Problemi della storia gallica in Italia', in *Hommages à A. Grenier*, III, Brussels–Berchem 1962, pp 1068–1094.

— 'Formazione delle civiltà storiche nella pianura padana orientale, Aspetti e problemi', *Studi Etruschi*, XXXIII (1965), pp 3–47.

— 'Etruschi e Celti nella valle del Po', in *Hommages à M. Renard*, II, Brussels 1969, pp 485–504.

Marzullo, A., *Le origini italiche e lo sviluppo letterario delle Atellane*, Modena 1956.

Mascioli, F., 'Anti-Roman and Pro-Italic Feeling in Italian Historiography', in *Romanic Review*, XXXII (1942), pp 366–384.

Mazzarino, S., *Dalla monarchia allo stato repubblicano*, Catania 1945.

— *Introduzione alle guerre puniche*, Catania 1947.

— *Fra oriente e occidente. Ricerche di storia greca arcaica*, Florence 1947.

— *Il pensiero storico classico*, Bari 1983 (2nd ed.)

Messerschmidt, F., see Duhn, F. von.

Metropoli e colonie di Magna Grecia (Atti del terzo Convegno di Studi sulla Magna Grecia, Taranto 1963), Naples 1964.

Meyer, E., 'Die Organisation der Italiker im Bundesgenossenkrieg', in *Historia*, VII (1958), pp 74–79.

Micali, G., *L'Italia avanti il dominio dei Romani*, Florence 1810; Florence 1821 (2nd ed.).

— *Storia degli antichi popoli italiani*, Florence 1832.

Momigliano, A., *L'opera dell'imperatore Claudio*, Florence 1932.

Mommsen, T., *Römische Geschichte*, 3 vols, Berlin 1854–1857, with later eds including Italian ed., *Storia di Roma antica*, Florence 1960.

Morel, J.-P., 'L'expansion phocéenne en Occident. Dix années de recherches (1966–1975)', in *Bulletin de Correspondence Hellénique*, XCIX (1975), pp 853–896.

Müller-Karpe, H., *Beiträge zur Chronologie der Urnenfeldzeit nördlich und südlich der Alpen*, 2 vols, Berlin 1959.

Napoli, M., *Civiltà della Magna Grecia*, Rome 1969.
Nenci, G., see *Bibliografia topografica della colonizzazione greca. . .*
Nissen, H., *Italische Landeskunde*, 2 vols, Berlin 1883–1902.
'Nuovi studi su Velia' (*La parola del passato*), 1970 (various authors).

Les origines de la république romaine (*Entretiens sur l'antiquité classique*, Hardt Foundation), Vandoeuvres–Geneva 1967 (contributions by various authors, on one aspect of the history of archaic Italy).

Pais, E., *Italia antica. Ricerche di storia e geografia storica*, Bologna 1922.
— *Storia dell'Italia antica*, Roma 1925.
Pallottino, M., see 'Scavi nel santuario etrusco di Pyrgi'.
— *Civiltà artistica etrusco-Italica*, Firenze 1971.
— 'Note sui documenti epigrafici rinvenuti nel santuario', in *Pyrgi. Scavi nel santuario etrusco (1959–1967)*, *Notizie degli scavi 1970*, II Supplement (1972), pp 730–743.
— *Saggi di antichità*, 3 vols, Rome 1979 (collection of previously published writings, of which the following are of particular relevance to the problems of Italy's pre-Roman history (date of original publication is given in brackets): 'Le origine storiche dei popoli italici' (1955); 'Appunti di protostoria latina ed etrusca' (1940); 'Sulla cronologia dell'età del bronzo finale e dell'età del ferro in Italia' (1960); 'L'origine des villes protohistoriques de l'Italie centrale' (1972); 'Nuovi studi sul problema delle origini etrusche (bilancio critico)' (1961); 'Le origini di Roma' (1960); 'Fatti e legende (moderne) sulla più antica storia di Roma: considerazioni critiche sulle scoperte e sulle discussioni più recenti' (1972); 'Tradizione etnica e realtà culturale dell'Etruria, Umbria e Romagna prima della unificazione augustea' (1940); 'Uno spiraglio di luce sulla storia etrusca: gli "elogia Tarquininensa"' (1950); 'Il filoetruschismo di Aristodemo e la data della fondazione di Capua' (1956); 'Gli Etruschi nell'Italia del nord: nuovi dati e nuove idee' (1962); 'Les relations entre les Étrusques et Carthage du VIIᵉ au IIIᵉ siècle avant J. C.: nouvelles données et essai de périodisation' (1963); 'Nuova luce sulla storia di Roma arcaica dalle lamine d'oro di Pyrgi' (1965); 'Rapporti tra Greci, Fenici, Etruschi ed altre popolazioni italiche alla luce delle nuove scoperte' (1966); 'La Magna Grecia e l'Etruria' (1968); 'La Sicilia fra l'Africa e l'Etruria: problemi storici e culturali' (1972); 'Servius Tullius, à la lumière des nouvelles découvertes archéologiques et épigraphiques' (1977); 'Sul concetto di storia italica' (1976); 'Nuovi spunti di ricerca sul tema della magistrature etrusche' (1955–56); 'Una mostra dell'Abruzzo arcaico e i problemi della civiltà italica medio-adriatica' (1970)).
— 'Internationale Beziehungen vom 9. bis zum 5. Jahrhundert v. Chr.', in *Kunst und Kultur Sardiniens vom Neolithikum bis zum Ende der Nuraghenzeit* (exhibition catalogue), Karlsruhe 1980, pp 180–184.

— *Genti e culture dell'Italia preromana*, Rome 1981.
— *Etruscologia* (7th series), 1984.
Panessa, G., see *Bibliografia topografica della colonizzazione greca*. . .
Paratore, E., *Virgilio*, Rome 1945.
Pareti, L., *Studi siciliani ed italioti*, 2 vols, Florence 1914.
— *Storia di Roma, I: L'Italia e Roma avanti il conflitto di Taranto*, Turin 1952.
— *Sicilia antica*, Palermo 1959.
La parola del passato, Naples (periodical containing articles, notes and commentaries concerned directly or indirectly with the history of pre-Roman Italy).
Pasquali, G., 'La grande Roma dei Tarquini', in *Terze pagine stravaganti*, Florence 1942, pp 1–24.
Patroni, G., *La preistoria (Storia politica d'Italia)*, Milan 1951 (2nd ed.).
Pellegrini, G. B., 'Popoli e lingue dell'Italia superiore', in *Centro Antichità Alto-Adriatiche*, IV (1973), pp 35–55.
Peroni, R., see *Italy before the Romans*. . .
Peyre, C., *La Cisalpine gauloise du IIIe au Ier siècle avant J.-C.*, Paris 1979.
Pfiffig, A. J., *Die Ausnreitung des römischen Städtewesens in Etrurien und die Frage der Unterwerfung der Etrusker*, Florence 1960.
Pisani, V., *Le lingue dell'Italia antica oltre il latino*, Turin 1964 (2nd ed.).
Poma, G., *Gli studi recenti sull'origine della repubblica romana*, Bologna 1974.
Popoli e civiltà dell'Italia antica, vols II–VII, Rome 1974–1978 (vols II–V of this extensive collective work contain discussions of pre-Roman Italy's cultural and ethnic groupings, with especial reference to their earliest development, contributed by various specialist authors. The sixth vol. concerns language and linguistics, and vol. VII contains essays offering an overview).
Prima Italia (exhibition catalogue, on the art and peoples of pre-Roman Italy), Brussels–Rome–Athens 1980–1981.
Pugliese Carratelli, G., *Scritti sul mondo antico*, Naples 1976 (collection of previously published articles, some of them more or less directly concerning the history of pre-Roman Italy: of particular interest are the following (date of first publication is given in brackets): 'Per la storia delle relazioni micenee con l'Italia' (1958); 'Achei nell'Etruria e nel Lazio?' (1962); 'Intorno alle lamine di Pyrgi' (1965); 'Lazio, Roma e Magna Grecia prima del secolo IV a.C.' (1968); 'Le vicende di Sibari e Thurii' (1974)).
Puglisi, S., *La civiltà appenninica*, Florence 1959.

Radke, G., '"Italia". Beobachtungen zu den Geschichte eines Landesnamens', in *Romanitas* (1967), pp 35–51.
Randall MacIver, *Italy before the Romans*, Oxford 1928.
Richter, G. M. A., *Ancient Italy*, Ann Arbor 1955.
Ridgway, D. and F. R. Ridgway, see *Italy before the Romans*. . .
— *L'alba della Magna Grecia*, Milan 1984.

Rix H., *Das etruskische Cognomen*, Wiesbaden 1963.
Rosenberg, A., *Der Staat der alten Italiker*, Berlin 1913.

Salmon, E. T., *Samnium and the Samnites*, Cambridge 1967.
Sartori, F., *Problemi di storia costituzionale italiota*, Rome 1953.
— 'La Magna Grecia e Roma', in *Archivio Storico per la Calabria e la Lucania*, XXVIII (1959), pp 183–188.
— 'Costituzioni italiote, italiche, etrusche', in *Studi clasice*, X (1969), pp 29–50.
'Scavi nel santuario etrusco di Pyrgi. Relazione preliminare della settima campagna, 1964, e scoperta di tre lamine d'oro inscritte in etrusco e in punico', in *Archeologia Classica*, XVI (1964), pp 49–117 (contributions by M. Pallottino, G. Colonna, G. Garbini, L. Vlad Borrelli).
Schulze, W., *Zur Geschichte lateinischer Eigennamen*, Göttingen 1904; repr. Berlin–Zürich–Dublin 1966.
Scullard, H. H., *The Etruscan Cities and Rome*, London 1967; 2nd. Italian ed., Milan 1977.
Sherwin-White, A. N., *The Roman Citizenship*, Oxford 1973 (2nd ed.).
La Sicilia antica, under the general editorship of E. Gabba and G. Vollet, 2 vols (in five bks), Naples 1980.
Sordi, M., *I rapporti romano-ceriti e l'origine della civitas sine suffragio*, Rome 1960.
— *Roma e i Sanniti nel IV secolo a. C.*, Bologna 1969.
Speranza, G., *Il Piceno dalle origini alla fine di ogni sua autonomia sotto Augusto*, Ancona 1934.
Studi Etruschi, Florence (annual specialist review, carrying the largest number of contributions on the civilisation not only of Etruria but of all the peoples of pre-Roman Italy).
'Studies in the Romanisation of Etruria' (*Acta Instituti Romani Finlandiae*) (essays by various authors), 5, 1975.
Susini, G., 'Aspectes de la romanisation de la Gaule Cispadane: chute et survivance des Celtes', *Comptes-rendus de l'Académie des Inscriptions et Belles Lettres*, 1965, pp 143–163.

Thèmes des recherches sur les villes antiques d'occident (Strasbourg colloquium, 1971), Paris 1977.
Thomsen, R., *The Italic Regions from Augustus to the Lombard Invasion*, Copenhagen 1947.
Tibiletti, G., 'La romanizzazione della Valle Padana', in *Civiltà romana nell'Italia settentrionale*, I, Bologna 1965, pp 23–36.
Torelli, M., 'Senatori etruschi della tarda repubblica e dell'impero', in *Dialoghi d'archeologia*, III (1969), pp 285–363; further material in *Arheološki Vestnik (Accademia Slovena)*, XXVIII (1977), pp 251–254.
— 'Per la storia dell'Etruria in età imperiale', in *Rivista di Filologia e di Istruzione Classica*, 1971, pp 489–501.

— 'La romanizzazione dei territori italici', in *La cultura italica* (Atti del Convegno della Società Italiana di Glottologia), Pisa 1978, pp 75–88.
— *Storia degli Etruschi*, Bari 1981.
Torelli. M. R., 'Tyrannoi', in *La parola del passato*, CLXV (1975), pp 417–433.
Treves, P., *Lo studio dell'antichità classica nell'Ottocento*, Milan–Naples 1962.
Trump, D. H., *Central and Southern Italy before Rome*, London 1966.

Vallet, G., *Rhégion et Zancle*, Paris 1958.
— see *Bibliografia topografica della colonizzazione greca*. . .
— see *La Sicilia antica*.
Van Berchem, D., 'Rome et le monde grècque au VIe siècle avant notre ère', in *Mélanges d'archéologie et d'histoire offerts à A. Piganiol*, II, Paris 1966, pp 739–748.
Van Compernolle, R., *Étude de chronologie et d'historiographie siciliotes*, Brussels–Rome 1960.
'Velia e i Focei in Occidente' (*La Parola del passato*), 1966 (various authors).
'Velia et les Phocéens. Un bilan dix ans après' (round table discussion, Centre J. Bérard), Naples 1981.
Ville, G., *La gladiature en Occident des origines à la mort de Domitien*, Paris–Rome 1981.
Vlad Borrelli, L., see 'Scavi nel santuario etrusco di Pyrgi'. . .

Whatmough, J., *The Foundations of Roman Italy*, London 1937.
Wikén, E., *Die Kunde der Hellenen von dem Lande und Völkern der Appeninenhalbinsel*, Lund 1937.
Wilamowitz-Moellendorf, U. von, 'Storia italica', in *Rivista di Filologia e Istruzione Classica*, n.s. IV (1926), pp 1–18 (also in *Kleine Schriften*, V, 1, 1937).
Wuilleumier, P., *Tarente*, Paris 1939.

Zuffa, M., *Scritti di archeologia*, Rome 1982 (collection of previously published articles, of which those most relevant to problems of *storia italica* are as follows (date of original publication is given in brackets): 'Scoperte e prospettive di protostoria nel Riminese' (1963); 'Le culture dell'Italia settentrionale all'inizio della conquista romana' (1964); 'Nuovi dati per la protostoria della Romagna Orientale' (1969); 'I commerci ateniesi in Adriatico e i metalli d'Etruria' (1975); 'I Galli sull'Adriatico' (1978)).

Additional Bibliography

A few general works on pre-Roman history have appeared since the original Italian edition of this book. Most of the studies, however, have been monographs given over to particular Italian populations or groups of populations rather than histories on a more comprehensive scale. Both type of study, however, have enriched and enlarged the perspectives offered in the original bibliography. Importantly, they include:

Bibliografia topografica della colonizzazione greca in Italia e nelle isole tirreniche, edited by G. Nenci and G. Vallet, III, IV, V: *Siti*, VI: *Opere di carattere generale, Addende*, Rome–Pisa 1984, 1985, 1987.
Celti ed Etruschi, Proceedings of the International Colloquium, Bologna, 1987.
Civiltà degli Etruschi, exhibition catalogue, edited by M. Christofani, Florence 1985.
De Juliis, E., *Gli Iapigi. Storia e civiltà della Puglia preromana*, Milan 1988.
Etruria e Lazio arcaico, conference proceedings, Journal of the Study Centre of the National Council of Etruscan–Italian Archaeological Researches, XV, Rome 1987.
Fogolari, G., Prosdocimi, A. L., *I Veneti antichi. Lingua e cultura*, Padua 1988.
The Imperialism of Mid-Republican Rome, edited by W. V. Harris, Proceedings of a conference, *Papers and Monographs of the American Academy in Rome*, XXXIX, 1984.
Italia omnium terrarum alumna. La civiltà dei Veneti, Reti, Liguri, Celti, Piceni, Umbri, Latini, Campani e Iapigi, Milan 1988.
Musti, D., *Strabone e la Magna Grecia. Città e popoli dell'Italia antica*, Padua, 1988.
Popoli e civiltà dell'Italia antica, VIII: Contribution by C. Ampolo, A. Bottini, P. G. Guzzo, Rome 1986.
Rasenna. Storia e civiltà degli Etruschi, Milan 1988.
Storia di Roma, I, *Roma in Italia*, Turin 1988.

References for each chapter are as follows, and are made to the above general list (author's surname and date of publication are given, or abbreviated titles in the case of collective works):

Publications of general interest: *Preface* and *Chapter 1*, 'Defining "Italic History"'.

Adriani 1968; Altheim 1941; *Atti V Congr. Intern. Studi Sicilia antica; Aufstieg Niedergang röm. Welt;* Beloch 1925; Bianchi Bandinelli 1973; Calderone 1955; Ciaceri 1927–1932; De Sanctis 1907–1923; Devoto, *Scritti minori* 1967, 1969; Ducati 1938; Duhn 1924–1939; Dunbabin 1948;

Furumark 1947; Gabba 1978; Gamurrini 1933–1936; *Le genti non greche della Magna Grecia*; Giannelli 1953; Göhler 1939; Heurgon 1961 (1979), 1969; Hofmann 1921; Homo 1953; *L'Italie préromaine*; *Italy before the Romans*; Klinger 1961; Langlotz 1968; Lepore 1963; Levi 1968; *La Magna Grecia e Roma*; Maiuri 1954, 1960; Mascioli 1942; Mazzarino 1945, *Fra oriente e occidente* 1947, 1983; Micali 1821, 1832; Momigliano 1966; Mommsen 1854–1857; Nissen 1883–1902; *Les origines de la république romaine*; Pais 1922, 1925; Pallottino 1971, 1972, 1979, 1981, 1984; Pareti 1952; *La parola del passato*; Pisani 1964; Poma 1974; *Popoli e civiltà dell'Italia antica*; *Prima Italia*; Radke 1967; Randall MacIver 1928; Richter 1955; Rix 1963; Rosenberg 1913; Sartori 1953, 1959, 1969; Schulze 1904; Scullard 1967; *La Sicilia antica*; Sordi 1960; *Studi Etruschi*; *Thèmes des recherches sur les villes antiques*; Thomsen 1947; Torelli, M. 1975, 1981; Treves 1962; Van Berchem 1966; Whatmough 1937; Wilamowitz 1926.

Chapter 2, 'Origins'.

Bérard 1957; *Il bronzo finale in Italia*; Casson 1959; Cianfarani 1978; *Civiltà del Lazio primitivo*; De Francisci 1959; Duhn 1924–1939; Franchi Dall'Orto 1978; Furumark 1947; *Le genti non greche della Magna Grecia*; Hencken 1968; Heurgon 1969; *Italy before the Romans*; Krahe 1949; La Regina 1978; *Magna Grecia e mondo miceneo*; Mansuelli 1965; Müller-Karpe 1959; Pallottino 1979, 1981, 1984; Patroni 1951; *Popoli e civiltà dell'Italia antica*; Pugliese Carratelli 1976; Puglisi 1959; *La Sicilia antica*; Speranza 1934; Trump 1966; Zuffa 1982.

Chapter 3, 'The flowering of Italy in the archaic period (8th–5th centuries BC)'.

Alföldi 1965; *Atti V Congr. Intern. Studi Sicilia antica*; Bérard 1957; *Bibliografia topografica della colonizzazione greca*; Braccesi 1977; Casson 1959; Ciaceri 1927–1932; Cianfarani 1978; Colonna 1974; De Francisci 1959; Dunbabin 1948; Franchi Dall'Orto 1978; *Le genti non greche della Magna Grecia*; Giannelli 1928; Heurgon 1969; *Italy before the Romans*; *Le lamine di Pyrgi*; Langlotz 1968; La Regina 1978; *La Magna Grecia e Roma in età arcaica*; Mansuelli 1962, 1965; Mazzarino 1945; *Metropoli e colonie di Magna Grecia*; Morel 1975; Napoli 1969; *Nuovi studi su Velia*; *Les origines de la république romaine*; Pallottino 1972, 1979, 1980; Pareti 1914, 1959; Pasquali 1942; Poma 1974; Pugliese Carratelli 1976; Ridgway 1984; Sartori 1953, 1959, 1969; 'Scavi nel santuario etrusco di Pyrgi'; *La Sicilia antica*; Vallet 1958; Van Berchem 1966; Van Compernolle 1960; 'Velia e i Focei'; 'Velia et les Phocéens'; Wikén 1937; Wuilleumier 1939.

Chapter 4, 'The Age of Crisis (5th–4th centuries BC)'.

Atti V Congr. Intern. Studi Sicilia antica; *Bibliografia topografica della colonizzazione greca*; Braccesi 1977; Casson 1959; Ciaceri 1927–1932;

Colonna 1974; Couissin 1930; Della Corte 1955–1956; Devoto 1967; Dunbabin 1948; Fogolari 1981; Frankfort 1959; *I Galli e l'Italia*; *Le genti non greche della Magna Grecia*; Giannelli 1928; Heurgon 1957, 1969; Kruta 1980, 1981; Lambrechts 1959; Langlotz 1968; Loicq 1978; Mansuelli 1962, 1965, 1969; Mazzarino, *Introduzione alle guerre puniche* 1947; Napoli 1969; Pallottino 1979; Pareti 1914, 1959; Salmon 1967; Sartori 1953, 1969; *La Sicilia antica*; Sordi 1960, 1969; Speranza 1934; Torelli, M. 1975; Torelli, M.R. 1975; Vallet 1958; Van Compernolle 1960; Wikén 1937; Wuilleumier 1939; Zuffa 1982.

Chapter 5, 'Roman unification and Italic continuity'.

Bernardini 1966; Brunt 1971; Couissin 1930; De Sanctis 1976; Devoto 1967; Felletti Maj 1977; Fogolari 1981; Frankfort 1959; Gabba 1954, 1971, 1978; *I Galli e l'Italia*; Göhler 1939; Harris 1971; Hatzfeld 1919; *Hellenismus in Mittelitalien*; Herbig 1942; Heurgon 1961 (1979); Ilari 1974; 'L'integrazione dell'Italia nello stato romano'; Kruta 1980, 1981; Lambrechts 1959; Lejeune 1977, 1978; Lepore 1963; Liou 1969; Loicq 1978; Marzullo 1956; Mazzarino, *Introduzione alle guerre puniche* 1947; Meyer 1958; Momigliano 1932; Paratore 1945; Peyre 1979; Pfiffig 1960; Rix 1963; Salmon 1967; Sartori 1969; Sherwin-White 1973; *La Sicilia antica*; Sordi 1969; 'Studies in the Romanization of Etruria'; Susini 1965; Thomsen 1947; Tibiletti 1965; Torelli, M. 1969 (and 1977), 1971, 1975, 1978; Torelli M. R., 1975; Ville 1981; Wuilleumier 1939; Zuffa 1982.

Acknowledgements

Photographic materials for the plates were supplied by the following institutions and collections:

Istituto di Archeologia e Antichità italiche dell'Università di Roma (Rome University, Archaeological Institute): 1, 2, 7a, 8a, 9, 10a, 11a, 12, 15, 16b, 17, 19, 20, 23, 24, 25b, 26, 28, 29, 30, 33, 34b, 35, 36.
Scala, Florence: 7b, 18, 31.
Vatican Museum (photographic archive): 6.
Deutsches Archäologisches Institut, Rome: 4, 8b, 11b, 13, 14, 32, 34a.
Electa Editrice, Milan: 27.
Leonard von Matt, Buochs (Switzerland): 10b.
Louvre, Department of Greek and Roman Antiquities (photograph: Maurice Chuzevoille): 16a, 22.
Soprintendenza Archeologica di Padova: 5.
Soprintendenza Archeologica di Bologna: 25a.
Professor Adriano La Regina: 21

Index